MY ALASKA!

A Memoir

NANCY LEE

Gotham Books

30 N Gould St.
Ste. 20820, Sheridan, WY 82801
https://gothambooksinc.com/

Phone: 1 (307) 464-7800

© 2024 *Nancy Lee*. All rights reserved.

No part of this book may be reproduced, stored in a retrieval system, or transmitted by any means without the written permission of the author.

Published by Gotham Books (July 25, 2024)

ISBN: 979-8-3302-9637-8 (H)
ISBN: 979-8-3302-9635-4 (P)
ISBN: 979-8-3302-9636-1 (E)

Because of the dynamic nature of the Internet, any web addresses or links contained in this book may have changed since publication and may no longer be valid.

The views expressed in this work are solely those of the author and do not necessarily reflect the views of the publisher, and the publisher hereby disclaims any responsibility for them.

DEDICATION

This book is dedicated to my friend and fellow Alaskan, Susan Tallman. I miss your common sense, wisdom, joy, and friendship. You are greatly missed by all who knew you.

I also dedicate this walk down memory lane to my greatest joy in this life: Andrew Lee and Melissa Lee, my wonderful son and daughter.

ACKNOWLEDGMENTS

I usually do not read Acknowledgments at the beginning of books, but now that I am writing my own I understand the gratefulness associated with it. Many people have been involved in the writing process, helping with fine details and grammar. My dear Mother paid for the transcription of stories I dictated on tape recorder. The typist involved stated that I "have the gift" and at times laughed so hard her coworkers stopped by to ask what was so funny.

She typed stories that had been written and sat gathering dust over twenty years. I sent a copy to a publisher and was amazed, they actually liked my book!

Ron Weber in San Antonio started the whole process by scanning my book and sending it all to the publisher. This was time consuming. Many thanks Ron. My sister-in-law Roni spent hours going through family photos since mine were in a frozen storage facility in Colorado. She provided me with great pictures to tell my story. She also assisted me with spelling and grammar.

Janie at Walgreens in San Antonio, Texas, was so helpful when I was there all the time printing photos for the book and asking a lot of questions. She was so patient and didn't hide when she saw me coming like some of the clerks did!

Mike Doyle also grew up in Alaska and was a constant support, buying me a much needed laptop and encouraging me to keep moving forward.

My main editorial guidance came from long time Alaskan friend Carol Brown. She was an inspiration.

My amazing big brother, Rev. Jim Hale kept me straight with details and provided words of wisdom. He just recently published his book about guiding high altitude climbers on Denali (Mt. McKinley) entitled *An Alaskan Lift of High Adventure*.

None of these stories would have happened apart from my brave parents, Dr. George and Mary Hale moving to the Territory of Alaska.

The territory eventually became the forty-ninth state of the United States of America.

CONTENTS

Dedication iii
Acknowledgments iv
Introduction vii
All Shook Up, The 1964 Alaskan Earthquake 1
What Do We Do Now? 5
How Did We Get There? 8
Smokey, My First Love 11
I Walk, Therefore I Ski! 16
Avalanche! 19
What Does Talkeetna Mean? 25
Our Piggy Misadventure 30
My First Cabin 33
Cabin Building or It's Raining In My House! 62
Gold Mining 69
Animals of Alaska 75
Airplanes 85
Trouble On The Mountain 93
Outhouses and Other Oddities 98
Last Thoughts 103

INTRODUCTION

I visited Alaska in 2008 for my Mother's memorial service and stayed with my son Andy in Anchorage. I woke up the first morning, turned on the local TV news and heard, "Several apartment residents awoke this morning to find a bear in their hallway." I knew I was home!

As I watched TV at a young age. I learned that Alaska was a misunderstood state. Yes, our fashions and television programs greatly differed from the "lower 48" states. Television film was flown by plane several weeks after airing in the states and current fashion could take years to reach our stores.

In 1950 my Mother took my brother John to visit family in Louisiana, the locals came knocking to see the redheaded Eskimo! I have actually spoken with folks that thought all Alaskans live in ice igloos. I am not kidding! Perhaps this erroneous concept is based on the location of our great state. One cannot drive to Alaska without traveling through beautiful Canada. The other is that Alaska is twice the size of Texas with many varying landscapes. Alaska has more coastline than the rest of the United States combined.

We boast of the highest point in North America, Mt. McKinley, (The Indian name is Denali, but when in Alaska it was always Mt. McKinley to me, I use them interchangeably). It has black sand beaches and turquoise ocean waters far from permanently frozen tundra. During the summer months' darkness is absent even at midnight. But during the winter, people suffer from lack of sunlight for six or more months. Natural resources abound and the animals are as large and diverse as the scenery. Come with me on a journey through a time gone by to My Alaska!

ALL SHOOK UP, THE 1964 ALASKAN EARTHQUAKE

It was a beautiful Good Friday, March 27, 1964. I was seven years old and roller skating in our basement with my friend Lisa. At 5:30 p.m. we stopped to watch Fireball XL5, oblivious to what was about to happen. Suddenly, the TV set began to glide from side to side, finally scooting away from the wall disconnecting itself from the electrical outlet.

Lisa alarmingly declared, "It must be an earthquake!" In a blink of an eye we were transported from the middle of the room ending up sitting against a padded bar. Miraculously, our position was the one place where we were protected from the shattering glass that flew across the darkened room.

Listening to the breaking glass above our heads we huddled together, giggling as kids are prone to do in an emergency situation. We watched fascinated as the tile floor rolled by like miniature ocean waves, popping up tiles as they sailed along. A roar like a freight train caused us to clap our hands over our ears. It was no longer fun! Then as quickly as it began, the earth quieted and an eerie silence descended. In the stillness we heard my Mother frantically screaming my name from upstairs. I heard the fear in her voice and realized something terrible had happened. We ran for the stairs, me with skates still on my feet but the clatter of the earth being torn asunder caused us to reconsider. The dancing stairway tossed us about like a carnival ride which made us laugh—oh, the bliss of ignorant youth! When the shaking stopped we hurried into the waiting arms of my Mother. My brother Jim joined us by the stairs holding his side after being tossed against a kitchen counter during the upheaval.

With a worried expression on his face Lisa's father appeared at our door. He was relieved to find her unharmed. Once he made sure everyone at our house was fine, he quickly retreated walking with Lisa in her pajamas. We were standing outside saying goodbye as my tall, lanky physician Father jogged down the street toward our house in

Bootlegger's Cove. He couldn't reach us due to a gaping twenty-foot crevasse in the paved road so he shouted across the fissure to see if we were all right. My oldest brother John was not with us. He was across town in an area called Turnagain with a friend, his condition was unknown because the telephones did not work.

Assured we were safe, my Father turned and ran back to the hospital to tend to the injured. He did not stop working on people's injuries for several days and nights.

Inside our house the pungent smell that ensued is one I shall never forget. The pantry had emptied itself onto the kitchen floor along with all the fine china and dishes. It was a peculiar odor of catsup, mustard, mayo, syrup, and whatever else had been on the shelves in breakable containers. A snow shovel was needed to scrape up the mess. Our house had been badly twisted, and we discovered that most everything breakable was either damaged or destroyed. The most bizarre example was my big brothers' trombone which the earthquake tied in a perfect knot! Neighbors checked on neighbors and men stopped by our house to check on us knowing dad was at the hospital. One neighbor took our relative's phone numbers and addresses to a ham radio operator. He contacted our distant family informing them we were safe. This was the only form of communication available and we were grateful for it.

Darkness. The crackling of the battery-powered radio and warm "mummy" sleeping bags kept us toasty warm that cold spring night. We hung blankets over the doorways to keep the heat inside. The fireplace and chimney had fallen out from the wall leaving a substantial gap which we tried to cover.

My Mother was reading a women's magazine by a kerosene Coleman lantern when flashing red lights and sirens cut the blackness. Mom ran to the door to investigate and came back furious. The emergency worker had told her to evacuate because a lethal tidal wave was predicted. My mom refused to leave our home in the darkness.

She said, "Absolutely not! We're not leaving!" After all, where would we go? The roads were impassable as far as we knew. We fell into a peaceful sleep lulled by the hiss of the Coleman lantern and we woke to no electricity, no working phones, and no running water. Gas leaks were a concern, and life in general would be a mess for some time to come. My young age protected me from understanding the seriousness of what was happening. I remember feeling proud of my Mother for her stubbornness in refusing to leave our home. I felt secure and safe that night camping in the living room. We found later that massive tidal waves did hit the state, wiping small towns off the map and leaving boats siting halfway up mountain sides. Fuel tanks and gas lines burned leaving a hellish landscape. Thankfully with all the damage there were few deaths.

The next day after the earthquake my brother John arrived home to a joyous celebration. He brought his friend to stay with us. People thought we lived in the safest part of town. Most of Turnagain By the Sea was now Turnagain in the sea. Turnagain was the hardest hit area in Anchorage with whole neighborhoods destroyed.

Boys being boys, my two older brothers and their friend were wrestling in the living room when a sound similar to a speeding train brought a sharp jolt to our house. We all ran quickly out the front door, one after the other, as fast as we could go. I was last in line and when I got to the top of our front door steps, a crystal clear thought came to me: *I'm going to jump as far as I can.* I jumped as hard as I could. Just as I did two feet of jaw-like crevasse opened up between the bottom step and the sidewalk. I soared right over it. If I hadn't jumped far enough, I would have fallen into it. By the time my feet hit the ground on the other side, the crevasse had closed, denied of a victim. I didn't see anything but poor Mom had a bird's-eye view standing on the top step with Ira Walker, a contractor friend. Ira was a gruff, wiry older man there to check on quake damage to the house. Mom's face turned white as freshly fallen snow.

When we all trooped back into the house I tried to reassure her, saying, "Don't worry Mom, it's just an. earthquake!" I had no idea what had just happened. Ira had dropped a thirty-foot metal measuring tape down an open fault in our yard and let it fall. He could not hear it hit, it was that deep. Ira showed me the break line in the cement where the fault had opened up when I jumped. I didn't really understand until later in my life. A huge crevasse had almost killed me. My Mother told me the story later with a faraway look on her face and I was amazed. Thinking it was my miracle most of my life, I realized later it was really for my Mother. She could not have lived after seeing her little girl crushed to death.

We left the house by nightfall the second night. We found out that one person was killed in a similar crevasse and another man had his legs crushed as the ground's gaping jaws grabbed him. He was with friends who dug him out quickly and got him to a hospital, saving his life.

I felt emotional leaving the house on the side of Cook Inlet. It had a beautiful view of Mt. McKinley and Sleeping Lady across the water. The authorities ordered us to remove the broken and twisted house from the property. Our house sat over one of the main faults that ran across the entire city and was rightly condemned. It sold for fifty dollars, the new owner had three weeks to move the house. The house was broken into three parts and the foundation was damaged. We were fortunate it didn't slide into the inlet like much of Anchorage did during the 9.2 earthquake. A 10 on the Richter Scale is total devastation. Our soil had just enough sand in the inlet clay to hold it together. My Father had come home for a quick sandwich that next day and we watched a small airplane fly by. It made the whole house shake like it was on top of Jell-O. Another good friend in town lost two children when their home slid into the sea; their bodies were never found.

Our house had been built during World War II and contained mysterious secret rooms. In my bedroom upstairs you could take the built-in chest of drawers out and crawl underneath into a small room. If you put the drawers back, no one could see you, they hid the room from sight. I had many good memories of my first home.

We did take the blackout shades with us. These were thick fabric window shades that kept light from being seen overhead by airplanes. In addition, they kept light out of bedrooms during short summer months when the sun seemed to never set, in the land of the Midnight Sun.

WHAT DO WE DO NOW?

Everything we owned went into big metal shipping containers because we had nowhere to go. There were no homes or apartments to be found in the city since all the available housing was snatched up immediately. Hundreds of people had been displaced. The day after the earthquake, Jim, Mom, and I packed what little we could fit into our tiny green Corvair, and we set out to stay temporarily with friends. John had returned to Turnagain with his friend.

The roads were passable around the crevasse. A dump truck and backhoe worked to fill the gap in the pavement that kept my Father from reaching us that first day. Jim and I were in the back seat of the car packed tightly by blankets and clothes. An official-looking man told us to pull over in a corner and wait until a huge semi-truck passed. It made no sense at all to wait because the road was clear ahead of us and the truck was far behind us. Mom argued with the man but this time decided to comply. We waited and waited, unsettled about sitting there so long. As the semi-truck navigated the corner, it contacted my side of the small Corvair, metal was slowly crumpling in toward me. We were being crushed, and no one was aware of it but us! The driver of the truck finally saw us in his mirror and stopped. He backed up until we were free and able to move. The official then waved us through. I had one mad Mama! In spite of the damage, our car still ran and made it safely to Dennis and Millie Branham's home. They were a childless couple who shared holidays and adventure trips with us.

They had no power or water either, but their house was intact. They invited our family to share their home. We melted snow over a camping stove for water and personal care. The fireplace was a popular place, cheery with its festive popping sound as the wood burned. I was either too hot or too cold and I found it difficult to get comfortable. To entertain myself, I tried over and over to ride atop their Great Dane named Trace. He was bony and difficult to ride. We moved on to stay with some other wonderful friends, Hans and Barbara Wagner. Hans had left Germany before WWII and come to America. He served as a member of the USA's elite military Tenth Mountain Division during WWII. He was also the 1964 Olympic Biathlon coach for our country. Their sons Chris and Hans Jr. were my brother's friends. It was close to Easter, so we girls set out to boil and decorate Easter eggs. I wrote on one egg, Thank You Jesus. Barbara showed it to my Mother who looked at me and could not speak.

From there we moved into a very, very small two-room house in Spenard (on the outskirts of Anchorage) that sat on a large dirt lot. We were lucky enough to rent it from the Branham's. Mom, Dad, the boys and I slept in one room. Mom and I slept in a twin bed and Dad and the boys in a roll-away bed next to us. In spite of the unrest (really, we were all so tired), Mom started her annual sweet peas, sprouting on a large cookie sheet with moist towels above and below the seeds. As they grew it was the only color I remember during that time when all seemed like a dreary black and white movie. The dirt outside easily became mud when it rained, keeping us from playing. When it was dry we played baseball and tracked in dirt for Mom to clean.

There were many earthquake aftershocks for some time which made us all freeze in place, holding our breath until they settled. Some aftershocks hit suddenly like a bolt of lightning while others would just linger for several minutes. Either way, we all reacted with the same tenseness until it was over.

School had started back up, but I got the mumps and was ill for three weeks which added to Mother's stress. Dad was only home to sleep and was house hunting while working long days. He had just paid off his medical office with complete lab, x-ray, and rehab equipment when the earthquake hit. Everything he had done in the building was destroyed. His office building stood at 501 L Street in Anchorage and remained their years after. I did go house hunting with him once, just to let Mom have some time alone as I recovered. I voted for the house with the swimming pool in it but that was not the one they chose.

The home my parents bought, with the help of a low-interest loan from the Red Cross, was a long way from town where we had lived. It was a country home for city folk. The roads were dirt and the population sparse. We had a "party line" or shared phone that all the neighbors would answer. Not all hung up if it wasn't for them. I left behind all my school chums. I had to make new friends which was really difficult. The families on Birch Road were large happy families that didn't need friends. I felt like an outsider and very alone.

The house we bought ended up having dry rot in three of the four walls and had to be rebuilt. We tried to unpack while living in a construction zone. It was all too much for my mom, having to deal with it all without my dad who was working feverishly to get his life and family back on track. The phone rang constantly at dinnertime, summoning Dad to the hospital. My oldest brother John was not home much being busy with his old friends and school—he had his own motorcycle.

It was all so challenging. The trauma of the earthquake affected our family in drastic ways. Pre-quake, we went to the Presbyterian Church most Sundays as a family. Saturdays in the winter, we spent swimming at The Spa, the only indoor swimming pool in Anchorage at that time. Another activity was skiing at Mt. Alyeska. Dad would get all of us and our equipment in the car and proclaim, "Off like a herd of turtles!" Inevitably, someone would forget something and we would have to turn back retrieving, hats, or other important items. We would sit around our fireplace at night, watching the flames dance while sitting on a bear rug that my Father had shot. I used to slide down the head of the bear while in diapers! We made homemade colas with carbonated water and Coke syrup while watching *The Ed Sullivan Show* in black and white on Sunday nights. I danced to the music and adults pretended not to see me. We were the Leave It to Beaver family. We had friends that played "kick the can" some nights, our favorite neighborhood game. We never wanted those games to end but eventually, one of our moms would call us in for bed. Our new home was on Birch Road, a small dirt road that gave me access to miles of unbroken fields for galloping a horse in the fresh mountain air. The *only* good thing about the move was that I got my first horse for my eighth birthday. He saved my life by becoming my best and only friend in the early lonely days after we moved. He was my first love. His name was Smokey.

HOW DID WE GET THERE?

Have you ever wondered what kind of person would want to make their life in Alaska? Well, I can tell you. They are strong, independent, opinionated, creative people who love challenge and adventure. Or folks who are running from something, like the law.

My Father, Doctor George Hale was a very handsome Navy Lieutenant (Junior Grade) aboard the USS *Alaska* during WWII. He was a surgeon who had operated after one Pacific battle for three days and three nights continuously. On his return to the States in 1945, he and my Mother Mary planned to head to China as medical missionaries. My Father had visited China after the war and fell in love with the people. He wanted to serve them in any way he could while my brave Mother was ready to follow Dad anywhere. But the communists began their takeover of the country by killing some of my parents' Christian acquaintances on the mission field. The Baptist mission board shut down all missions one month before the date of my parents' departure. The door to China was forever closed for them.

Dad had completed his surgical residency at Washington General Hospital in D.C. Totally by chance, my Father came across a man in a diner who was the owner of the new Alaska Railroad. The man had asked if he could sit at Father's table, and they started a conversation. He told Dad that the railroad needed a surgeon in Anchorage, Alaska. At that time there wasn't a surgeon to be found above Juneau in southeast Alaska. People in need of serious medical care had to be flown to Seattle or Juneau. A doctor was needed in Anchorage to triage the injuries for the state rail system and to direct all the care and decide where to send people for treatment, including Anchorage. Having been raised in Missouri and Minnesota my dad loved to hunt and fish. He and Mom ventured into the untamed new Alaska territory where he became the Assistant Chief Surgeon for the Alaska Railroad.

At that time, Anchorage was a huge military tent base for the Army and Air Force. Fourth Avenue was the only paved street. The military had created a road out of the mud and tundra from Seattle to Fairbanks called the Alcan Highway. It crossed through breathtaking Canada into Alaska, now a very nice road for access to Alaska by vehicle. It took many years for it to be easily driven.

After working for the railroad Dad eventually started his own private surgical practice. He hated the disease of cancer and the havoc it wreaked on people's lives. He was highly involved with the American Cancer Society and was a much loved and respected force in the state. When he was 73 years old, 400 of his patients and coworkers attended his retirement party. My brother sang "Oh Lord, It's Hard to Be Humble" to a laughing appreciative audience, including my Father who always enjoyed a good joke. He was a strikingly handsome man, tall and fit, much like the actor Charlton Heston.

I have a vivid memory of an Austrian man who had come to Alaska just to find Dad. They were sitting in the living room quietly chatting when I walked in. The man told me, "Your Father saved my life." He took off his shoes and socks, revealing scars on both heels. His ship had taken a direct hit by a Japanese bomb which imploded, collapsing the decks one on top of the other. He had been crushed in between the folding decks and his leg bones were forced through his feet. My Father had operated on him and saved his life.

That was a familiar story to me growing up. I still meet people who will respectfully tell me that Dad had saved their lives or the life of a loved one. I never tire of hearing it. My Father had tremendous self-control and integrity. The only time I ever saw him cuss or get extremely angry was once when I had tied my spooky horse Smokey to a tree with a slip knot around his neck—I certainly gave him good reason!

Dad didn't speak much about the war as his generation did. One day with tears in his eyes, he told me that his beloved Battle Cruiser the USS *Alaska* had been sold after the war to make razor blades. Years later Dad was honored to tour the nuclear submarine named for his revered ship.

Dad went to medical school at Harvard, paid for by family friends that believed in his potential. His Father was a third generation Baptist preacher who lended his pulpit to his son on occasion. My Father's nickname around the hospital was The Deacon, referring to his discipline in the operating room. He was a voracious reader and kept his Operating Room at a certain humidity and temperature because it reduced infection. He was not only a surgeon in the community; people brought their children to him for counseling. People of all colors and walks of life loved my wise and compassionate Father. He was the most colorblind person I have ever known, treating every person with absolute compassion and respect.

My Mother was a spitfire of a gal raised by a widowed Mother during the Depression. She obtained her Bachelor and Master's Degree in English and Music Education at Louisiana State University. My parents met at a Southern Baptist student convention. While my Mother was speaking, Dad turned to his friend and told him, "I am going to marry that girl." He did! Once in Alaska, Mom became a powerful advocate for the arts and directed her Presbyterian church choir. She taught at the only high school in early Anchorage and founded the Alaska Festival of Music which brought performing arts talent to Alaska. While directing the Anchorage Community Chorus she worked with Bing Crosby and Bob Hope on their televised Christmas shows. She received an Honorary Doctorate Degree from University of Alaska, Fairbanks. While working for the University of Alaska it was said, "Before you call Washington, call Mary Hale". She knew how to get things accomplished! Mom was extremely tender-hearted, and we teased her often for her sensitive tears. She was moved deeply by small things while possessing a wonderful sense of humor. She was the most compassionate person I have ever known, showing empathy toward people and animals.

My parents lived happily in Anchorage from 1949 until my Father's death in 1999. They were true pioneers who blazed a trail for culture and progress across the wilderness that was Alaska.

SMOKEY, MY FIRST LOVE

What do you say about one's first love? It was exciting just to be together. We explored and learned so many new things. He was always fun to be with, alert for danger and protective of me. Let me tell you my first and forever love story.

I had been horse crazy my entire life, all eight years of it! We owned many horses over the years, but the best one was Smokey. He didn't arrive Smokey, he came to me as Grizzly, a horse that been free on the Canadian range. He was unwilling to be caught, didn't like to be ridden, jumped sideways at the least provocation, and bucked me off daily.

After the earthquake we had a home with sufficient acreage to keep a horse. My parents contacted friends Johnny and Marge Gibbons. John had been a rugged, handsome cowboy horse wrangler in Hollywood where he met his starlet wife Marge. Margie was vivacious and sassy; John a quiet storyteller. He always had a funny story to tell from his many experiences over the years and was good company. He would draw on his stories to illustrate a horsemanship lesson or something he wanted to teach me. John was a true horse whisperer, a very patient and knowledgeable horseman.

There I was on my eighth birthday waiting breathlessly with my heart pounding in my chest for my dream horse to arrive. John was riding him to our house. I heard his quick step before I saw him. He pranced right into my heart that day, with his head up, ears forward, and eyes, taking in the scene. He was the most beautiful dapple-gray horse I'd ever seen. A steed he was, but the name Grizzly just didn't fit him. Discussing names one night, my mom came up with Smokey, which totally fit. And Smokey it was. He was a big, powerful, six-year-old Percheron with a quarter Thoroughbred, which made him fast as the wind.

John had made a bet with our wily Contractor Ira Walker one day. There was a large spruce tree stump that had to be pulled out and removed in our back yard. Ira bet John money that Smokey could not pull it out; it would take a bulldozer. The next day neighbors showed up to watch the competition. John mounted Smokey and threw a lasso around the stump. Smokey pulled it straight on without much result and everyone laughed, they thought it couldn't be done. Then John tried from a different angle. Smokey powered up his hind haunches, dug in and pulled until the stump slowly rose to the surface. My horse hauled it off with the crowds' jaws falling. It got very quiet with the bulldozer sitting silent, the neighbors went home.

Smokey had feet as big as pie plates, shoes had to be ordered ahead of time because of the large size. He didn't like me much at first, bucking me off every day for weeks to prove it. Afterward he would stand ten feet away with his head down in repentance; I stopped crying or tried to catch my breath after landing on my back and getting the wind knocked out of me. Smokey figured out that no matter how many times he bucked me off, I was just going to crawl back on. I was just as stubborn as he was! I think he finally gave up. John wrote a poem for me, but I only remember the first few lines:

> Here sits Miss Nancy of Birch,
> Upon her most perilous perch,
> A horse named Smokey with fire in his eye,
> She said, "I'm as safe as if sitting in church!"

He would jump at even a leaf blowing across the dirt, and I learned to be ever ready for his sudden detours. The first time I tried to saddle him by myself, he bolted away. He was caught by a man in the mountains behind our house. My saddle had slipped underneath his belly but was still cinched. Johnny Gibbons rode him home and I got a mounting block with steps so I could carry my saddle to the top, putting it on easily. I was so tiny it helped a lot! I could do this with the front pasture gate closed so if the horse did get away, he could not go far.

I usually brushed him and hopped on bareback without a saddle and off we'd go. When I rode bareback people asked me to get off and watch me get back on. They reported I crawled up Smokey's front leg to get on. I grabbed some mane and swung up. I never understood what the big deal was until much later when I saw my daughter get on her ranch horse Jasper bareback. She crawled up his leg! I knew then what they were talking about, very cool to watch! Right leg swings up and left leg wraps around the horse's front leg and inches up. Odd that both my daughter and I got on our horse the same way! When I tamed Smokey, or he tamed me—I don't know which—we finally became best friends.

Alaska had no fancy horses, just good, average, solid and strong ones. We rode everywhere, all day long into the night in the summer. I rode Smokey so much bareback that his sides had indentations where my legs rested. I loved the wind in my hair and he loved to canter, off we would go where the bear and moose played! There were no constraints, no fences, or subdivisions, just places to explore. And we did it together.

He got his first barn and stall. He looked around like he couldn't believe it and slowly stepped inside. He felt like a king. He never pooped in that barn, ever. I think that was the start of him knowing he was loved and had a home. His eyes grew softer and he quit bucking me off. I was just a little redheaded flea on his back but he started tolerating me. Johnny found out Smokey was bucking me off and took him for a ride. When he came back he told me Smokey would never buck me off again. I don't know what he did or said to the horse but he never bucked again. Ever.

He didn't like to be caught. I would feed him then sneak soundlessly under the front gate behind the barn, and close the pasture gate before he ran out. He was always listening, so it was a race to the gate. But I usually won because eventually he had to eat. Early on when he first arrived I ran out barefoot to catch him. As he ran by I got him by the mane while trying to undo the rope that held the gate which kept him in. He had this wicked look in his eye and ever so slowly positioned his steel-shod front foot over mine. Then he put it on top of my small foot and leaned on it with all his considerable weight. All I could do was scream and pound his shoulder with my fists until he moved, resulting in a swollen, bruised foot. He still wanted to let me know who was boss.

One time, he took the bit between his teeth and ran toward home without me able to stop him. The western bit I was using had a high center which most likely hurt him. After that I rode him with a hackamore bit which he liked. He could eat grass, and I could control him. I rode him in the State Fair that year and won my first blue ribbon and trophy. He had really tamed down! The next year I started jumping. I'd ride Smokey into the show ring to jump and people would just die laughing. The ground would shake as he cantered between fences. He was a huge draft horse and nobody thought he could get off the ground but by golly, he did! He would do anything for me. I won my first silver cup on Smokey in jumping. I had several learning disabilities. After a day of failures in school I would ride for a few minutes and the stress would fall away. Smokey listened to all my problems.

No horse loved me like he did. When we rode I would talk to him about anything and everything. He always had one ear turned back to me listening; the other listening ahead for anything dangerous. In the summer I often found him sleeping in a sunny spot and would go lie down on him and we napped, just the two of us.

We had a baby colt born in our pasture. I was looking for the mare when Smokey came running through the pasture, whinnying. He led me to the mare that was just giving birth. We both watched in reverence and amazement as she dropped and cleaned her baby. Such a friend he was! He was a constant presence in the pasture, running, bucking, and snorting with the cold wind and snow flying under his feet. I hopped on, bareback, sitting on thick, frozen icicles that dripped down his sides in winter and we would fly through the deep fresh snow. He grew a six-inch coat in winter to keep warm in the minus thirty-degree weather. The snow builds up inside the horse's hooves like big snowballs, requiring us to stop and pick them out. When I needed fun, adventure, or just a listening ear, Smokey was there for me.

In the short summer months, we would ride on small roads or paths through the vibrant green forest; the thick, sweet smell of the woods rich mosses and lavender tea bushes filled my senses. We rode up mountains, in town and horse shows with the ever present horseflies, gnats, and mosquitoes to accompany us! When I went away to college in Oregon, I called John Gibbons because I knew Smokey was lonely in the pasture all by himself. John came out and took him to a cattle ranch off Kodiak Island on the Aleutian Chain. The island, Sitkaletic, experienced mild weather enabling the horses and cattle to graze year round. One day they brought a stallion onto the island to populate the herd. Smokey immediately broke down the corral and ran him into the ocean. The people rescued the stallion and built corrals especially for him, but at night when they were asleep, Smokey came and tore the corral down again and ran the stallion back into the water. He wasn't going to have anything to do with that horse! Smokey was large and in charge!

That cattle ranch later failed. I had heard through the grapevine that Smokey had died, which made me wonder how and why. I had the opportunity to visit the island in the spring of 1993. Smokey had a half brother and sister that had lived on that island into their thirties but were killed in the tidal wave as a result the 1964 earthquake. It was a most beautiful place—soft mountains of waving grass surrounded by crystal blue ocean. I pictured my friend happily galloping with his herd across the hills, wind in his mane, fresh ocean air in his lungs. The caretaker of the lodge told me that when the horses were brought across on a flat open barge, killer whales jumped up trying to grab them. The report I choose to believe said Smokey died by a little lake to the side of the lodge where he sunned himself in the afternoon. I also heard that mink farmer on the island later shot all the horses to feed his mink. The mink farm failed.

I WALK, THEREFORE I SKI!

As an Alaskan I grew up on skis. One of my earliest memories is of skiing Mt. Alyeska outside of Anchorage at the age of four. Using a rope tow that ran up a little hill in front of the ski lodge; I skied with no poles thinking I was really fast. Each time I skied faster. Once, I looked up to see a man standing in front of me. I looked up and couldn't figure out how he got there. He said, "Oh, you're awake. You had a pretty bad fall and laid there for a while; I thought I'd check to see if you were all right." I don't know who he was, but I was glad he came to check on me. I had knocked myself out cold. I got up carrying my little skis into the lodge and rested, telling no one in my family what had happened to me.

I took skiing lessons which I absolutely hated. No matter how cold or horrible the weather, we skied. Everyone else in the class skied better than I could. I made sitzmarks in the snow when I fell or dug my tips into the big bumps needing someone else to dig me out. I do remember burying my ski tips into the middle of a bump and just bouncing there like a cartoon character. I had one friend in ski class who always dug me out when my skis stuck in the huge "moguls." I shivered unable to move my feet. These big bumps would soften in the sun then freeze again in the afternoon making a big slippery slide. Now they groom hills by flattening these bumps. The girl who stopped to dig me out was my angel spending much time rescuing me. I am sorry to say I do not remember her name. So often the rest of class would ski on to the warm lodge and leave us, but she never left me alone and did not ski off until I was free to ski myself. I skied Mt. Alyeska top to bottom from the time I was five years old.

At the end of the ski lessons, all thirty kids entered a big ski school race. I heard that same little voice that had instructed me to jump as far as I could during the earthquake. I told myself, *I'm going to go as fast as I can*. And I did—I won the race much to my instructor's surprise.

Perplexed, she bought her worst student a candy bar for winning, a ten-cent candy bar never tasted so good!

Both of my brothers were no less than fantastic on skis. My big football playing brother John was fourth in the Junior Nationals when he was a teenager. He went on to college and pursued other interests, not ski racing anymore. It was amazing to watch him float down a hill. He was 1968 senior class president at Dimond High School, a dynamic guy who later went into broadcasting and politics. Being a bit of a fun loving prankster, his closest friends remembered him most for his integrity. I knew him as a protective older brother who was always there when I needed him. My middle brother Jim, was extremely popular—everyone loved him, they still do. He has a grace with people that my Father had—open and compassionate. In school he ran cross country, track, and skied, even trying ski jumping. He became a hang glider enthusiast and mountain climber. He flew with the late Don Sheldon, one of Alaska's aviation legends and later started his own mountain climbing and guide business on Mt. McKinley. I have to thank him for hauling me along on his adventures, teaching me to rappel down rock cliffs, kayak, rock climb, self-arrest on a glacier, and water ski. Ultimately Jim became a Pastor in Talkeetna, Alaska and later left Alaska to pastor a church in Grand Junction, Colorado. He is now a missionary to Peru and goes every two years to visit and preach. He also authored an excellent book about his climbing exploits: *An Alaskan Life of High Adventure*.

I really didn't fit into my family of athletes and achievers. My brother John even told me so, "You just don't seem to fit in this family." I was painfully shy and backwards. My social skills were poor, I managed to be a little to the front when everyone was in the back, or to the left when everyone else went right. Whining worked on my Mother so I figured it would work on everyone, wrong! I didn't do well in school and hated it. My stomach ties in a knot still when faced with a test. I had many learning disorders that were never diagnosed as a child, people in their frustration with trying to teach me told me I was lazy and stupid! I would learn a math concept and sleep erased it. I had such anxiety that mistakes piled up creating more disappointment and failure. I believed what they told me while trying so hard to do well.

I loved being on my horse outdoors with the wind in my face and red hair streaming behind me. No one could tell me I was stupid or lazy there—it was my safe place. Smokey was always my safe place.

Though my early school career was tenuous, I did later graduate Summa Cum Laude with my Associate of Arts degree from Matanuska-Susitna Community College, University of Alaska, Palmer. Proving to myself I was NOT stupid, I walked across the stage to receive my Bachelor of Science, Nursing degree, from Mesa State College, Grand Junction, Colorado in 1996.

AVALANCHE!

I preface the following story with an amazing fact to give the reader indications of the excellent physical condition of my Father, Dr. George E. Hale. At eighty years of age he ran a 10k race. Although he finished last, he ran in to a standing ovation from all the runners. He was proudly escorted by with two police cars behind with their lights flashing. It was a glorious sight and provided us all with a wonderful memory as he never ran again.

My Father experienced earthquakes, avalanches, cancer, airplane crashes, and survived them all. He is a perfect example of the stamina, endurance and determination demonstrated by Alaskan men.

Avalanche is a scary word. The White Death steals precious lives that should not end so tragically. Dad and my brother John experienced this terrifying ordeal, after which Dad wrote the following story:

> March of 1963, friends invited the Hale family to spend a weekend at Rainy Pass Lodge on Puntilla Lake in the Alaska Range of mountains to explore the possibilities of skiing in the area. Mary and I along with Johnny age 12 Jimmy, age 9, and Nancy age 6, were flown the 140 miles to the lodge in two ski equipped airplanes. One was a 4-place Helio Courier which is a very high performance short takeoff and landing plane and the other a 4-place Taylor Craft piloted respectively by Dennis and Jimmy Branham. On a beautiful Friday afternoon, we flew by 20,320-foot Mt. Mckinley and many other beautiful, rugged snow covered mountains on the way. The next day while John and Jim hunted ptarmigan and snowshoe rabbits on snowshoes with son of the lodge caretaker, Dennis and I loaded my skis and poles into the Helio Courier, and took off. We flew around in the mountains with tops flat enough to land on, good slopes for skiing and a suitable landing area near the bottom. Eventually we landed in a small bowl at 5,400 feet near the top of a mountain about 3 miles from the lodge. We unloaded my skis and poles and after Dennis had taken off and climbed away without

mishap, I climbed on skis to the 6,000-foot peak of the mountain above the bowl where we had landed. Then I skied down into the bowl and down a ravine running toward the lodge. Eventually I came to a steep narrow 7-foot-wide chute bounded by vertical walls of sharp rocks. As I skied down the chute the tips and tails of my skis scraped the rocks at the sides. Below the chute I stopped and looked back hoping to find a better course around the chute. As I looked up the mountain I saw a long steep ravine to my left filled with smooth powder snow which led into the ravine where I was standing. There was a big cliff between the two ski runs but above the cliff was a large shoulder like ridge covered by smooth wind packed snow. I decided that if I should ski this slope again I would traverse across that shoulder and ski down that beautiful powder snow instead of scraping my skis on the rocks forming the sides of this chute. I then skied on down the ravine worked my way through a tangle of Alders in the creek bottom skirted a ridge to the left, skied down a hill and frozen snow across Puntilla Lake and arrived at the lodge. Sunday morning the temperature was 17 degrees partly sunny and partly overcast, Johnny and I planned to ski together. Jimmy preferred to hunt with the caretaker's son again and I encouraged this not wanting all of the male members of the family to be landing on mountains in the same airplane. This was fortunate since I don't believe a boy of 9 could have survived the day. After breakfast, Johnny and I loaded Dennis's plane, and took off and flew around the mountains again looking for another good run to ski. The air was rough and we could find no other satisfactory mountain so we eventually decided to try the same one I had skied the day before. Since there were some rocks protruding through the snow where we had landed, Dennis wanted to land in his tracks of the previous day, not having scraped the plane's skis on rocks in the landing or take off. We approached the mountain bowl about a dozen times but kept going around due to the turbulence and the overcast, which resulted in whiteout conditions the previous day's tracks in the snow could not be seen in time to land smoothly. Johnny was almost air stick by the time we saw the tracks early enough in the approach for Dennis to land with the skis back in the grooves of the previous day. Johnny and I unloaded our equipment, put on our skis, took some 8mm movies, and began our descent down the gorge. Dennis had a movie camera and took pictures from above as we began our descent. We had another camera with us and took pictures of each other occasionally. We began to warm up, seemingly from the exertion and took off our outer jackets and put them into a rucksack I was wearing to keep from getting wet with sweat. When we were just above the narrow chute I had skied the previous day we turned right and began our traverse across the steep shoulder as I had planned. Suddenly we heard a loud crack above us. We looked up to see what was coming down on us and immediately discovered that the entire area of the shoulder, which had been covered by an 18' slab of wind packed snow, was sliding fast with us standing in the middle of it. We plummeted down a very steep sixty-degree slope, sliding with the snow between sharp rocks projecting three to four feet above the snow and dropped over the brink of the cliff. We fell through space, completely blinded by the falling snow, for what seemed like an hour. Finally, I thought, *Aren't we ever going to hit?* Just then, we crashed glancing off of a steep bank of crusted snow. I hit on my right back side, feeling a sharp snap in the ribs of the left front part of my chest and in my lower back. My ribcage had broken open like a dropped watermelon, and I felt sure my low back was injured. Then we floated down a steep gorge in the avalanche. I found myself swimming instinctively and desperately with long powerful surfacing strokes trying to keep my head above the snow. Large blocks of snow were sailing silently down the gorge over my head confirming other observations that avalanches travel like a caterpillar tread, faster on top and slower on the bottom due to surface friction. Suddenly and mercifully, the avalanche stopped. My head was above the surface of the snow! The rest of me was buried in a shallow grave of snow. I stood up, throwing off the snow and was free. My ski bindings had released and the safety straps attaching them to my boots had broken in the fall but my ski pole straps were still around my wrists. I looked around and down the gorge and found that I was entirely alone—there was no sign or sound of Johnny. He had vanished entirely I said, "Oh God, no!" I was badly injured and the gorge was filled with many tons of snow. Statistically fifty percent of people buried in avalanches are dead within thirty minutes and ninety-seven percent in an hour so there was no time to spare! I had no idea where John was but he had been below me when the avalanche started so I walked down the surface of the avalanche feeling and hearing my broken bones grinding with a very unpleasant sound like a loud kerwhump with every step. But mercifully, I was still too numb to feel pain. Suddenly I heard a voice from under the snow say, "Get me out of here fast!" I picked up a large block of crusted snow about 2 feet square by 18" thick at random, and discovered it was right on top of John's racing helmeted head. He was completely locked in the snow and was able to breathe and talk but otherwise could not move even a finger. While carefully excavating him I discovered that he had apparently been knocked out by the fall remembering only the loud crack at the start of the avalanche. He woke up being unable to see or move, but hearing the crunch of my steps down the avalanche surface above him. Probably his racing helmet had saved his life. After Johnny was released he seemed to have only a sprained ankle and thumb. He commented, "This makes you feel a little shaky doesn't it?" I heartily agreed. We started to walk but with each step my foot would break through and sink about nine inches into the snow and my ribs would dislocate with the loud grinding kerwhump so I found myself completely immobilized where I stood. Johnny took the movie camera and made a quick sequence of the fault remaining above the shoulder over the cliff where the slab of snow had separated; the approximately fifty-foot cliff; the surface of the avalanche with the shallow grave where I had stopped with my skis being visible beneath the snow; the place where he had been entombed; and me standing and dumping the snow out of my pockets. Needless to say it had penetrated everywhere, filling my clothes and my pockets too. Johnny climbed up the avalanche retrieved my skis, and put them on for me since I was almost helpless. Then I noticed that my sunglasses were missing. Johnny made another trip up the avalanche and found them buried in the snow where I had surfaced. With my skis in place, I stayed on top of the snow instead of sinking into it. My bones displaced much less frequently and I was able to travel again. We left as soon as possible since I wanted to get as far as I could before the blessed numbness wore off of my fractures. We skied on down the ravine and I tried stemming as much as possible and lightening my skis as little as possible in turning, to avoid displacing my fractured bones. By the time we were down to the tangle of Alders in the creek bottom, I began to feel pain and couldn't suppress a few loud groans when my skis became entangled resulting in falls. Since skiing is a one person operation Johnny could not help at all so I told him to ski back to the lodge and tell the others what had happened and that I was hurt but would make it back in. By the time Johnny arrived at the lodge, Dennis had become concerned over the delay and was about to fly out to look for us. I eventually worked my way through the tangle of Alders, climbed over the ridge, skied down the hill across the lake and arrived at the lodge. We soon learned that the temperature had risen from 17 degrees when we took off that morning to 48 degrees in a few hours and the rapid warming had loosened the snow, resulting in the avalanche being triggered by our weight. I had my friends tie a triangular bandage tightly around my chest, and took a couple of stiff pain killing drinks of whiskey. Then Dennis and Jim flew us back to Anchorage. After x-rays at Providence Hospital indicated that I had at least three fractured ribs and a fracture of the cartilage margin holding the rib cage together, we went home. The next morning in spite of medicines I woke with pain at 3:30 am. Thinking that I might be in less pain sitting up, I tried for half an hour to get up by myself in order not to interrupt my wife's peaceful sleep. No matter how I turned or maneuvered I couldn't get up, so finally I had to wake my wife Mary Helen and ask for a lift. For the rest of that week I couldn't get out of bed without help, but once up I was able to get around. That Monday I had an eight o'clock operation scheduled which I performed but for some reason I didn't help lift the patient from the operating table to the stretcher after the procedure was completed. At noon, as was my custom I walked the 7 blocks downtown from my office to the

Chamber of Commerce luncheon. After working that week seeing only very essential patients I spent the next week at Mt. Alyeska Ski Area as the Chief Surgeon for the National Alpine Skiing Championship. Skiing was tempting but after taking one ride up the main chairlift and finding that it hurt even when the chair bumped gently as it passed over the pulleys of the towers, I decided against it. The next week I resumed full practice. A month after the avalanche, I was in a sporting goods store I had passed while walking downtown the day after the accident. One of the employees said, "I had just returned to Anchorage after an absence of 4 years, saw you walk by slowly all hunched over looking pale and grim and thought Dr. Hale sure has aged in the last 4 years!" Four weeks after the avalanche, I was again skiing cautiously but enthusiastically at Mount Alyeska. Johnny was not only skiing wildly as usual but spent a beautiful warm sunny afternoon skiing down the south face of the mountain across the valley floor up a sharp ridge and sailing 150 feet through the air. He passed by 15 to 20 feet over my head with his clothes flapping in the wind. What a recovery!

John had arrived long before Dad, informing everyone of the avalanche and Dad's injuries. I remember they all ran out to help Dad get across the frozen lake. John and I were left sitting in the main log cabin at Rainy Pass Lodge. John moved his thumb up and down making the fractured bones grind, "Isn't that cool?" he said.

Many years later, my Father was experiencing severe low back pain and had an x-ray. It showed he had broken his back in the avalanche and cartilage had grown around the fractured vertebra to stabilize it. My Father was skiing one month after the accident with a fractured spine and didn't even know it!

This was typical of Alaskans—they're tough, determined folks. One of my Father's sayings was, "The Good Lord took a likin' to me!" And I know that was true.

WHAT DOES TALKEETNA MEAN?

On a beautiful brilliant Alaskan summer day in 1979, I daydreamed while in a college class. I was partially listening to the professor expound on things that weren't going to move my soul or impact my life. I asked myself the question, *Nancy, if you had one year to live, what would you do?* I knew one of the answers was, *I wouldn't be sitting here in a college class.* I thought about that question a lot and the realization came to me that I wanted a simple life and to be in the tiny village of Talkeetna. I didn't know all the reasons; I felt it was time to move.

A job opened up in the little museum and a house became available. The house was fifty dollars per month consisting of two tiny rooms and a bathroom. The job paid five hundred a month; I gratefully accepted them. It was quite a miracle for those to open up in a village of 250 people. I took it as a sign.

Talkeetna is a nice, funny little place. It had 4 bars, 4 churches and 5 great places to eat. One small grocery store had milk and canned goods called the B+K Grocery. It burned down twice and was not rebuilt. It was a staple for us in the 80's. An airstrip cuts across the middle of town by the museum. A wheelbarrow holds a classic sign, "Welcome to Beautiful Downtown Talkeetna!"

My older brother Jim and his wife Roni had just moved to Talkeetna where the large rivers of the Talkeetna and Chulitna join the Big Susitna River. Talkeetna is a native word meaning "Where three rivers meet."

While attending church on Sundays I started noticing a guy by the name of Don. On Sundays I'd see him come in to church, not exactly the prince charming I would have picked out, but there was something that really drew me to him despite his unkempt appearance. His long dark brown hair looked like it had been cut with a knife in chunks, and he had serious beard stubble. He wore torn mud-splattered flannel shirts, no deodorant, hip boots, he was gnarly. On the positive side, he was tall, wiry, and very muscular with sweet brown eyes. I found out that he built the cabin he lived in with his younger brothers Robert and David plus a few other friends from Minnesota. They drove a little Datsun pickup to church with the guys sitting in the back of the truck. There was no real road, so when they'd come to a bad mud puddle they'd all get out in their rubber hip boots, pick the car up, and walk through the muddy spot. That road provided us with many interesting experiences in the years to come.

Looking out the museum window where I worked, onto the village airstrip, I spied on Don at his plane. I would run to the back window of the museum to get a better view. Little did I know, he used to pee behind his little cabin not far away before taking off. Good thing there were some hardy trees between me and him!

I purposely got the mail about the time he landed and one day I was nonchalantly walking by hearing, "Hey! Come back here!" I looked up as a pig ran at me! It was rather odd because this was the middle of winter with the temperature only ten degrees above zero. The pig had really sparse hair as pigs do, but each hair was about seven inches long—I'd never seen anything like it! I found out his name was Mr. Pig and Don had acquired him from Stephan Lake Lodge where this pig had survived the winter. Don caught him and put him in the back seat of his Super Cub. The pig rode in the small plane as if a paying passenger enjoying his flight to Talkeetna. Although he was pretty tame, it took seven men to wrestle him down and hold him in the Ahkio sled behind the snow machine to transport him to the cabin. I guess he considered snow sleds scarier than flying!

Sometimes I saw many interesting things outside the museum window. One morning I saw Don driving by on the snow machine. In the Ahkio sled behind him sat a big reclining easy-chair with his brother David sitting in that chair like a king. It was a pretty funny sight making me laugh.

Another time, I witnessed a sled dog team running down the street next to the runway full blast; a fantastic sight—ten beautiful dogs strung out. They really do love to run; it's in their breeding. Right behind them came another dog team obviously out of control. The driver was leaning on his brake and snow flew twenty feet in the air while he was cussing up a storm. They were trying to catch that first team. Dog fights happen between teams and the dogs get horribly tangled in the harnesses, it's a true hot bloody mess costing some dogs their lives. Sometimes sled dogs do what they want to do! It's in the breeding. From my museum vantage point I saw it all. I saw everything that went on in that little village by the river.

That spring Don was flying out to Stephan Lake Lodge where he worked, to open it up for the summer season. I invited myself to go along. The lodge was about forty miles northeast of Talkeetna, a rustic log fortress situated on a reflective mirror-like lake. On the way we flew over three grizzly bears, a mama and two cubs. As Don circled the plane so we could view them better, the enormous mama reared up on her hind legs pawing and swiping at the plane. She was willing to take on a plane twice her size. I knew at that moment where the term "mama bear" came from. She was going to protect those cubs at her own risk. I do believe had we been any closer she would have brought our plane down. She was that powerful. Her demeanor made our plane seem very small. What an incredible sight!

When we arrived at the lodge, Don offered to make me a cup of hot chocolate. Don as the caretaker lived there alone for several years. When you're out in the Alaskan bush by yourself you learn to make do with what you have. I had no idea what I was getting when I got the hot chocolate. All I knew was it did not look like hot chocolate nor did it taste like hot chocolate. Don drank his right down but I politely declined. Suspicious, I went into the kitchen and discovered he had taken some chocolate cake mix and dumped it in hot water! Ick!

Don had a hunting guide license. With that and his Super Cub, he was able to go anywhere he wanted to. Super Cubs are high performance two seater small planes known for their ability to take off and land in a very short distance, like river sandbars. Don's plane had soft, oversized tires called tundra tires that made it easier to land on uneven surfaces.

I flew with him one day to pick up camp equipment left behind after the hunters were flown out.

On top of a 7,000-foot mountain in the Talkeetna Range Don had set up a sheep hunting camp. Alaska is not for the faint of heart. Don was one of the few pilots to land on top of mountains in the Talkeetna

Mountain Range. It's amazing when you are three minutes away from smashing into a granite mountain, how close you get to God. To put this in perspective, when you're riding in the back seat of a Super Cub, you're behind the pilot. The pilot has a much better view of what's going on but sitting in the back seat you see things from a totally different perspective. It's much like a man driving a car with the woman sitting in the passenger seat—different perspective. If everyone in this world flew little planes in Alaska, God would have a lot of company. So there I was, with my different perspective seeing nothing but solid rock mountain looming out the front window. I was crying out loud, "Oh God! Oh God!" My eyes shut, I hung on. As we touched down Don applied the throttle because the "runway" was a little uphill. Urgently slamming my tense body into the left side of the fabric plane we whipped around on the mountaintop—to park. Don hopped out with ease as I peeled my hands from the seat. When I extricated myself from the plane I was met with a deafening silence. I tire at the overuse of that word, but standing there looking to forever and hearing the noise of nothing was truly awesome! I was miles from people or anything of man's creation—no cars, no airplanes, no trains, not even animal noises—just God's untouched world. The silence roared in my ears, swirling and moving like the wind. There really are no words to describe it. I was experiencing Holiness.

Standing on that mountain I vowed to come back and experience it again. We couldn't stay there forever, although I wanted to. As we loaded the tents and gear into the plane, Don explained that we would free fall a bit before the plane built up enough air under the wings to fly. *Okay, I can do that*, I thought as I was buckling my seatbelt. Don pushed the plane back as far as it would go to give us more room to takeoff, I was fine. He got in, hit the little cross he had hanging overhead and said, "Here we go! Hang on!" The plane rolled downhill at full throttle, bouncing off the mountain. The ground ran out, and we literally fell off that mountain straight down for *hours*. I screamed. I screamed until the gracious Lord in heaven above saw fit to have that airplane, *inches* from the valley floor where I planned to die, lift its little nose and slowly rise. Up we flew. I was still screaming. Don calmly said, "What's the matter? We had a hundred feet left."

Our relationship progressed (I did finally stop screaming) and the night before we were to be married, Don brought me back a wedding present from a hunting camp—a round, fuzzy Golden Retriever pup who barked constantly. We named him Boomer but had no idea what to do with him because we were leaving for our honeymoon. My sister-in-law Roni kept Boomer for us. His exciting exploits will be covered in chapters to come. He turned out to be the best present ever.

For our honeymoon we loaded up the Super Cub with me still wearing my wedding dress and flew into Anchorage. We hadn't really told anyone where we were going but as soon as we walked into the hotel room the phone rang. Don picked it up and it was the Federal Aviation Administration wondering why we hadn't closed our flight plan. If a flight plan is not closed it could mean a plane was down and a search party would be launched. Don hung up the phone and gave me the funniest look. He said, "Those guys can find me anywhere!"

OUR PIGGY MISADVENTURE

Don came from Minnesota and when we visited his home state, I found I liked it. I favored the country hobby farms, which had little white houses and red barns. In Alaska we didn't have a little white house—we had our cabin—and we didn't have any barn, but we had a woodshed.

Trying to be thrifty we decided along with our neighbors the Parkers to raise a couple of wiener pigs. With freezer occupancy in mind for them we made a deal to buy two piglets. The Parkers would feed them and keep them at their place. Feed, water, eat, easy. I didn't know anything about pigs when I went to pick them up. While parked in the driveway a horrible odor assaulted my senses. I couldn't believe the smell. The farmer put two piglets into a burlap bag with a knot at the top for transport. It was a hot day and I drove the stinky, pooping, squealing pair in the back seat of my little Toyota Corolla for two and a half hours. By the time I got to Talkeetna, my head was out the window and I was driving as fast as I could go! Don was flying for a local air taxi and as I went by the airfield, I yelled out the window, "Take the pigs!" Don put them in the back of his truck. By that time a hole had been chewed in the burlap sack and their little heads were poking out. I had no idea a pig could do that! I don't think I ever got that awful smell out of my car! They sure were cute but we had no idea what we were in for. The two pigs refused to stay in their pen at the Parkers; they kept coming over to my house about a quarter mile away. They had a particular fondness for fresh garden food and if they weren't in the Parkers garden, they were in mine. At that time neither household had running water or electricity. We pumped water and hauled it by hand to our gardens—a lot of hard work. With choice words being said, pigs' nostrils flaring, brooms waving, the dog barking—it was crazy times around our place chasing pigs. I wanted to kill them early!

One day after finding them in my garden, I turned Boomer loose, and we rounded them up and into a ten-by-twelve-foot woodshed. I quickly tried to build up a barricade of firewood to block the entrance thinking I could keep the growing pigs in the woodshed. When I went in the house these crazy things would hit the wood with their noses, knock it down then hop over the top; going back to happily munching my garden. What kinds of pigs do that? Boomer and I went outside again, rounded them back up with my broom and got them into the woodshed. The pigs turned it into quite a game. After the fifth episode I was becoming a little angry. Giving them a lecture, I told them in no uncertain terms that I didn't like what they were doing. I don't think I was very nice about it. Satisfied, I bent over and started to put my stack of wood back up when something whammed me right in the fanny! It felt like a freight train had hit me and I almost went sprawling face down. I turned around and there was a defiant little pig, his nostrils flaring. He'd goosed me right in the rump! Really, what kind of pig does that? I learned never to take my eyes off of them. We opened the door and let Boomer go get the pigs, but Boomer was a Golden Retriever, not being a very intelligent pig-herding dog, chased them back home instead of running them back to Parker's! I sneaked up on them with my broom and wailed the tar out of them! You can't hurt a pig—they're indestructible! The pigs were impossible to keep fenced in and we got pretty tired of them coming over. We discussed just leaving them in the garden.

One night I had to get Don's help. He lassoed one of them by the leg and tied it in the back of his pickup. The poor thing struggled while screaming at the top of its lungs making all sorts of racket. It was deafening. The other pig ran madly around and around the truck trying to find his partner. Don tried to tackle it. Boomer barked making the pig run faster. We tried everything we knew to no avail. After a two-hour fiasco reminiscent of the Keystone Cops, Don finally lassoed it. He put the pig in the truck hotfooting it to our dear neighbors' house. There was nothing I could do to help because these pigs were getting big and they were much too strong for me. I watched from the truck while Don steered them back to their pen one at a time by their hind legs; like pushing a screaming struggling wheelbarrow. By that time the seat of his pants had ripped out flapping open with each step exposing his cheeks. He was covered in mud, not to mention, mad! I nearly died laughing! With every step, his pants would flap and just send me off.

We were all so happy when it came time to butcher those pigs. We had a party. The Parkers killed and bled them and we brought ours home to butcher. The pig was stiff with its feet sticking straight out, its mouth open and head covered with dried blood. We hung it right inside the front door on our little bit of entry way linoleum. Its head and legs were reaching out toward the front door. As soon as we got it hung up and were ready to start butchering, we heard footsteps and whistling. It was our good friend John Timmers. He didn't bother to knock because he saw both our cars in the driveway. Don snickered saying, "Shh, shh, don't say anything." John opened the door and looked up into the face of that hideous pig. He quickly stepped back letting the door shut. He stood there for about fifteen minutes shaking and repeating over and over, "What the world?" I don't think he ever forgave us for that. We laughed until we cried at the humorous ending to our wild and crazy piggy adventure. What kind of people do that?

MY FIRST CABIN

One of the most interesting ventures during our life in Alaska was building log homes. Our first log home was unique, to say the least. It was half log and half used cardboard from the local grocery store. Don didn't have a lot of money but he had his two brothers and three roommates to help build.

Prior to our wedding we upgraded the plywood floor to carpet with linoleum in the entryway and small kitchen. One night we heard a snow machine slicing through the still winter air from a long way off. The front door exploded open and a headlight illuminated the cabin. In came a snow machine. It was Don's younger brother David who came to visit. He stayed for a cup of tea. Leaving, he grabbed the back of the heavy machine turning it around, opened the front door, pull started his machine, and with a cloud of exhaust went into the night. I mopped up all the water that melted on the entryway floor.

The next day through the rumor mill I heard that David was upset and said that he had ruined the cabin! All the bachelors drove their snow machines in the cabin to mechanic them. The plywood floor was forgiving but now it was changed forever by carpet. I am sorry David!

After all those bachelors had lived there for several years, I was more than a little apprehensive about moving in. They cleaned it up really well for me. One day when I peeked into a bottom kitchen cupboard, a glint of light off a glass object stirred my curiosity. I reached in pulling a gallon jar from the back. I set the jar on the counter and started gagging. The jar was full of mouse tails and feet. The mice had fallen in the jar and could not get out, to stay alive they ate each other. Gross. Rodents are a big problem when you live out in the woods.

Besides mice our cabin hosted a resident weasel. He was beautiful; silky brown in the summer. He was a weasel, small head and long muscled body with a long wiry tail. I named him Herman, Herman the ermine. He thought he was the boss of that cabin until he met me. He once had taken on big six foot two John Timmers over a sandwich John was making. The ermine won! The greedy animal hauled the sandwich behind the counter but couldn't get it outside. It sat rotting after all that trouble.

I walked in one day and Herman the ermine decided he was going to show me who was the boss—after all, he was there first! He was a frightening sight standing defiantly on my kitchen counter and spitting at me! He only weighed one pound but I suppose it was his wildness that caught me off guard. No one in my twenty-six years had ever taught me how to handle a spitting ermine. I didn't know whether to run or to kill him. He was a fierce little bugger and although I got the broom out, I decided not to mess with him that time. He finally had enough of me, quit the standoff and retreated into the woods. He never came back into the cabin while I was in the kitchen. What a little gentleman!

One of our wedding gifts was a beautiful glass candy dish with a lid on it. We filled it our first Christmas with yummy homemade fudge—a pound of it. That night we heard the top of the candy dish slide off and we knew precisely who the culprit was. The next morning, we came downstairs to an empty candy dish. The fudge was gone! We caught sight of the little bandit later that day and he was so fat he could hardly move. He had to push his stomach up off the ground with his back foot in order to move forward. That was the last we ever saw of our greedy little ermine. Death by chocolate. We missed him terribly.

We had other animal visitors to our cabin in the woods. We noticed very large bear tracks in our driveway every spring and summer. Since our cabin was located by a large river, the bears would come by for a salmon snack. Driving to town one day we saw three little heads in the river poke up like periscopes; it was river otters checking out their surroundings. We also saw red fox, moose, and all sorts of birds.

After living in a real home most of my life, I now found myself in a primitive cabin. During the winter Don would go away to work leaving me with what is known as "green wood." This is fresh cut and too wet to burn. I sat in front of the fire in my boots and my coat all day long—blowing, puffing, and praying, trying to keep the fire going in our old barrel stove. Sure enough about four o'clock it would finally get going, and by five o'clock when Don came home it was nice and warm in the house.

The wood burning stove we had was an old barrel full of shotgun holes with a door on one end and a chimney on the other. It produced too much heat then no heat at all. When too hot, we removed the plastic sheeting from the windows upstairs. There was no glass in the windows. When it was too cold, we wore boots, hats, and gloves inside. I'd mop the linoleum floors and then skate in my slippers on the ice that formed. Our kitchen floor was somewhat slanted and I'd get a running start on the carpet grabbing the countertop and hanging on for dear life to keep my feet from slipping back down. While standing upstairs I could actually tell which way the wind was blowing. With that kind of setup, it was impossible to keep the mosquitoes out in the summer. One mosquito can keep a person up all night. Miserable.

We did have a bathtub that drained outside. To use it, water was heated up in buckets on the wood stove and the cooking stove. A ton of work but so nice! I only used it twice. We took hot showers at the local Laundromat; otherwise we did what my Mom called *spit baths*.

We lived in a very fertile area that had once been river bottom with wonderful soil. That first summer I decided to plant a garden. Great idea, except for the fact we had no running water. Never one to do things in a small way; when Don made my garden, he made it big. I went ahead and planted the whole thing with cold climate vegetables: cabbage, carrots, lettuce, beets and potatoes to name a few. I hauled water. Chickweed took over the entire garden and there was no way I could win the battle of the weeds. My Mother's garden in Anchorage was always beautiful and weed free but she couldn't keep the moose out of it. She tried Irish Spring Soap, human hair, and even an electric fence! Nothing worked.

That fall I visited several of the farms in the Matanuska Susitna Valley. I picked vegetables to bring home and can because my garden didn't produce anything edible. I really enjoy home canned food—it tastes so good, and it's actually fun to prepare. That year wasn't fun. I had to hand pump the water from the pump in the kitchen, boil it, and then wash the jars and food, fill the jars then pressure cook them. It really made me appreciate running water! It took about three times as long as it would have with that convenience, but I did it. The food turned out fine but I'm not sure I'd ever want to do it again. However, knowing that I'm capable of the task made the experience worthwhile.

In the winter this food would sometimes freeze, but we ate it anyway and it was just fine. We fished for salmon and received moose roadkill every year. Yep, I said roadkill. The State Troopers kept a list and when a moose was hit by a car or train, people on the list would be called to go pick up the meat. Nothing would go to waste. People hauled the animal home and butchered it, always thankful for the delicious protein. Once Don went to pick up our moose and it wasn't there, just a trail of blood. Don followed it to a nearby cabin and asked for the moose back. The moose thief was new to the area, saw a dead moose and took it home unaware of the list. Moose is a wonderful healthy lean meat. Because of that list we always had meat to eat. We kept a freezer in town for our meats and frozen food. In winter we put several packages of meat in a cooler at home. It was cold enough to keep them frozen.

We came home one night finding pieces of white butcher paper all over the yard. We saw no saran wrap that we wrapped the meat with before applying the butcher paper. Boomer looked a little guilty but it was a mystery. When he would not eat after several days we took him to the vet. One x-ray showed us who ate the meat. Boomer was full of saran wrap! He had digested the large pieces of meat. We let him naturally pass the saran wrap becoming his old self. He never ate our meat again!

We did finally get running water. It consisted of a little twelve-volt pump that would pump water up into a 300-gallon tank that sat upstairs in our cabin. From there gravity fed water to the faucet in the sink. It worked pretty well. We ran the pump off a car battery; it seemed that when you needed it the most, the battery would run out of power.

One winter night darkness fell and Don wasn't back. It was getting late, about 9:00 p.m. While he was gone I watched a wonderful TV show about a nurse, and the suspense was building. I love the field of medicine, it was very exciting to me. I wanted to see this show, and at the same time, I kept wondering where Don was. He usually gives me a call when he's late via a patient friend and neighbor Chris Mahay. She would relay messages to me using the Citizens Band Radio or CB. That night, as my program got to the best part, the TV began to dim as the car battery failed. Chris was probably trying to call me on the CB with a message from Don, but that did not work either because the battery ran out. I spent the dark night alone hoping Don was safe. Don came home the next day, he had been weathered in and had to put the plane down for the night. Bad weather can build quickly and make flying unsafe. Sometimes the weather closes in all around you. Pilots have to land and wait it out. You always carry survival gear—at least a sleeping bag for every person and matches. My friend Sharon who flew a lot in small planes said, "I never get in a plane without my toothbrush and a pair of clean underwear!" I was with her once when we got weathered in, landing and camping in an old abandoned cabin for shelter overnight. She had her toothbrush and fresh undies! When someone does not make it back, you hope its weather and not a crash. We lost many friends each year while flying in bad weather and during hunting season.

Dr. George and Mary Hale reunited after a two-year tour with the Pacific Fleet during WWII. Behind is Dr. Hale's Battle Cruiser, the USS Alaska. He was the first one off the ship.

Mary Hale in hunting camp late 1940's. She shot a caribou that wandered into camp and cried for hours. She never hunted again.

Mary Hale attempting to ski, she eventually fractured her shoulder and became a "lodge bunny". Notice the Cubko binding and lace up boots.

Mary Hale conducted the Anchorage Community Chorus, far left in evening gown.

Mary also directed her Presbyterian Church Choir.

The Hale family Christmas card photo from 1962. The fireplace and chimney behind fell out of the wall during the 1964 Alaskan earthquake. Photo by Harry Groom.

Dr. George Hale at "Hale Lake" where he had total access to the salmon in the lake for over twenty years. He swore everyone to secrecy about the location of the lake. You could catch your limit of salmon in twenty minutes. Totally ruined me for fishing anywhere else for life! Photo by Jim Hale.

"The World's Best Supercub" on floats at Christiansen Lake, Talkeetna, Alaska. George had a custom IFR (Instrument Flight Reference) equipped panel put in his plane so he could fly safely in clouds or fog if needed. Most small planes are VFR (Visual Flight Reference) creating risk in bad weather conditions.

Nancy Hale at nine years of age barrel racing her beloved horse Smokey at Fort Richardson, Alaska 1965.

Nancy and Roni Hale ocean kayaking Katchemak Bay, Homer, Alaska. Photographed on the Homer "Spit" in front of the Salty Dawg Saloon. This was Roni's handmade and duct tape patched river kayak. What an adventure we had!

Every girl's dream, to ride a horse on a beach. Especially Alaskan girl's! 1985 San Diego, California Roni and Nancy lived a dream. After the first canter down the ocean beach, we both had tears streaming down our faces. Photo of Nancy by Roni Hale.

Nancy and mountain guide brother Jim Hale at "the beach" on the Susitna River circa 1982. Dig those glasses! Photo by Roni Hale.

Cousins Crystal Hale, Andy Lee, and Jonathan Hale in their first cross-country ski race, Talkeetna, Alaska. Photo by Roni Hale.

The Bird House was a cabin turned into a popular dive bar along the Turnigan Arm. It burned in 1996 and is sorely missed. Photo by Mike Doyle.

Don Lee using a "come-along" while building a log cabin at remote Papa Bear Lake, Alaska.

This is a gold plant operating in Kantishna, Alaska. It is a two story high sluice box that enables miners to dig deeper along creeks for gold. The small yellow plate across the conveyor belt trapped a miner nearly taking his life.

Cousins Michael Hale and Missy Lee at Dr. George and Mary Hale's 50th wedding anniversary. They would both summit Mt. McKinley together in 2005. The expedition was led by Jim Hale.

This was taken of John Hale and his beautiful wife Deena Tsiatsos-Hale camping in Southeast Alaska the summer prior to their fatal airplane accident in 1982.

Any Lee running through Glenwood Colorado with the Salt Lake City Olympic flame. He had torn his ACL and both meniscus in one knee prior to the run.

Melissa (Missy) Lee at 17,200-foot camp on Mt. McKinley with Mt. Foraker in background. She summited the highest point on North America with her uncle Jim Hale leading what other climbers called "the Family Group". She later climbed the highest peak in South America, Mt. Aconcagua.

Missy, Nancy, and Andy Lee at Mary Hale's memorial service in Anchorage, Alaska 2008. The Presbyterian Choir and Anchorage Community Chorus both sang that day in tribute to their early conductor.

Dr. George E. Hale's triumphant triathlon teammates. George, right swam; George Etsel biked; and Marcie Trent ran. Marcie was later killed by a bear while running up a popular hiking trail.

Andy Lee, lifelong Alaskan on a fly-in fishing trip. He is shown here with a Northern Pike and is a catch and release fisherman only.

Nancy and navigator Daisy her rescue dog paddle on Enoch Lake in Colorado.

CABIN BUILDING OR IT'S RAINING IN MY HOUSE!

After all the trials and tribulations of living in our rustic cabin, we had come to the conclusion we needed conveniences since I was pregnant with our first child. We bought a beautiful piece of raw land on Christiansen Lake, Talkeetna. We went to work clearing the trees. Most folks can't even relate to building a house from raw land. After Don had gone in and cut down all the trees with a chainsaw, we had to clear them off the lot. We rented a crane to pull them out. My job was to sit in the little cab on the vehicle surrounded with clouds of carbon monoxide. Racing the motor increased the carbon monoxide while pulling logs off the property. I was getting sick and lightheaded. The bugs were awful—every tree that we moved sent up a flurry of mosquitoes and gnats which would eventually fly into the cab where I sat.

The neighbor's cat liked all other dogs but our Boomer. The cat loved to ambush and terrorize poor Boomer every chance he could. The last we saw of Boomer that day was his backside as he ran through the woods as fast as he could go, ears flat back, a wild look in his eye with the cat firmly attached spread eagle and growling to his side!

I had my baby Andy in October but still had no place to live. We were out of the old cabin with no home ready to move into. I stayed at my parents for three weeks while Don was busily constructing our new home. We had a cinder block basement set into the side of the hill with windows and doors. Don had applied tar paper to the flat roof and laid pressboard on the floor by the time I joined him there. We didn't have sheetrock on the walls—all we saw was the beautiful silver and pink insulation. There were no interior walls so I hung sheets. We had one functioning sink in our bathroom when we moved in. I had my running water, electricity, and telephone, that's all I cared about. I was glad to be home!

Little did we know at the time but a flat roof was hard to live with! Although that winter was a cozy one we had a few leaks here and there and mice troubles galore. Don chased them with a broom as they ran between the plastic sheeting and insulation on the ceiling. He even shot one with his .22 pistol. It was an interesting winter. The highlight of the year for me was taking an Emergency Medical Technician class. I will always thank God that I was able to learn those useful skills. They would be valuable the rest of my life.

We returned from a spring of employment in Anchorage to a badly damaged basement. Somehow water had started pouring in our bedroom window and soaked everything. When we arrived home, Don's sister Jody came to spend the night with us. She threw her sleeping bag down on the floor right outside Andy's room. It had been raining hard for several days, and the flat roof held no more water. The rainwater came through the roof materials and into our home. By the time we awoke the only dry places in the basement were where we slept. Everything else was a dripping mess. Pretty soon I ran out of pots and pans to collect it all. Son Andy, still in diapers, was having a great time playing in it however. At first I tried to keep him out of the water because of the fiberglass but it was a losing proposition. When Jody woke the next morning all she heard was *drip, drip, clunk* when a raindrop hit a pan. That morning it was literally raining in our house—you couldn't walk anywhere without getting wet.

Not five minutes after Jody got up and picked up her sleeping bag the whole ceiling above her tore loose and gushed torrents of water. She came running into our room, screaming, "You wouldn't believe what just happened!" I took one look at the mess and decided maybe it would be best to leave. At that point my Mother called to ask how things were going. With all these loud drips in the background, I lied as I stood there, "Fine, Mom, everything is just fine." After I hung up the phone I called my sister-in-law, Roni. They planned to be leaving for three days and said, "Come on over, stay here." I packed up the suitcase, looked at Don, and said, "I'm leaving. You can come with me if you want." There was nothing for him to do but follow.

It took him three days with a big heater to dry out the basement. Once dry, we moved back into the basement with hope of no more rain. After being wet the pressboard floor swelled up, splintered and broke up, leaving ugly concrete patches. Andy would be covered in sawdust every night. I still had my good sheets up for walls and it was always a little embarrassing when someone had to use the bathroom. My sister-in-law from Minnesota, Janet came to visit for Don's sister Susan's wedding. She had never been to Alaska before this trip. After being in our unfinished houses, she sat quietly in my house for a little while with a thoughtful look on her face. Finally, she said, "Don't people here have walls?" I had to explain to her that a lot of the houses in Alaska are built as money becomes available. In that way we avoid big mortgages, but don't have the most glamorous of living situations for a few years. It's amazing how you get attached to that crazy silver and pink *wallpaper*.

The logs finally went up several years later in thirty-degree weather. Thankfully the mild temperatures held during that winter. Don was working while there was daylight and had an assortment of friends to help out while learning to do log work. He had also hired the Mannix brothers, Chris and Arthur, who were artists at log work.

The huge logs shook the whole house when they were rolled into place. Chainsaws buzzed overhead like giant bees carving out the wood. Thank goodness the chainsaws only cut wood and no humans!

Chainsaw injuries can be serious, even life-threatening. I was a bit afraid one of those monster logs would fall right through the roof into the basement but none did, which made me very happy. The blessed roof went up!

By the time the roof was on I was pregnant again with our daughter Melissa We really wanted to finish the interior of the basement before the baby arrived. A few thousand dollars came in unexpectedly and we hoped to use it to finish the interior of the basement. I had dreamed for two years about having sheetrocked walls and carpeted floors. In my dreams I had pictured the baby's room finished, wallpapered, clothes washed, and ready for a baby, so I could come home from the hospital and relax. Things simply did not happen that way. We decided the best way to redo the basement was to muck out the house, that is, take everything out so we could work unhindered. Our bedroom had been sheetrocked, covering up all the silver insulation and we were painting it. I had to stop every so often and take a breather, being very pregnant. The first night we were asleep on our rollaway bed because we had taken everything out of our house, creating a huge pile in the front yard.

Then it happened—three weeks early. I kept thinking. *No, this can't be!* Don drove us to the Anchorage Providence Hospital. It's normally a two-and–a-half-hour drive, but he shaved off an hour. I had our baby girl Melissa. When I got out of the hospital with Melissa we came straight back to Talkeetna. Since my house was still being worked on, I stayed in my brother's little guest cabin nearby. My sister-in-law Roni had worked really hard to make the small cabin cozy and inviting. I had no running water to help with a two-year-old in diapers and a brand new baby but I knew how to deal with it because I had learned in our first cabin. I used water from red plastic gas cans and kept the woodstove going with a pan on it for warm water.

I was that grateful that I had a place to go to with some privacy to start getting acquainted with my new baby and be with toddler Andy. The ladies from church brought me a meal every night so I didn't have to cook dinner. It was really wonderful of them to do that. Meanwhile, I'd go over and console Don, trying to encourage him. When you're building a house, it seems like it will never get done.

Six years later we still didn't have cupboard doors and we still lived in the basement, but our house was paid for! We lived about eighty miles from the nearest large grocery store, bank, and any major convenience. It was a three-hour round trip in good weather. We did have a small store in Talkeetna called the B & K that sold essentials. That winter in our basement was one of the coldest in history, with horrific windstorms plummeting the chill factor (the current temperature combined with the wind-chill effect) to 80 degrees below zero! We stored up our food every summer for the hard-to-travel winter months. That year when the cold hit we didn't have to go anywhere because of our own storehouse. We nestled down inside our warm and cozy little basement with our new wood stove blazing away.

In the summertime our dog Boomer would escort Andy to the sandbox daily. Andy would grab the fur on boomer's back and go play. Don "wore a lot of hats" during our married life. He was bush pilot, gold miner, cabin builder, and carpenter.

One of our cabin building episodes took us to Papa Bear Lake, outside Talkeetna, one summer. The children were a little older and more mobile. Instead of Don leaving to work on the job we decided to take the kids and make these three weeks' family time. There was a little plywood shack where I could cook with a nice outhouse, a bonus on any Alaskan's homestead! Every day I would try to divide my time up into various activities, but it seemed like all I did was cook and eat! I put on five pounds even though I was active. I took the kids out for rides in the rowboat every day and Donny made them toys. I kept a journal of the daily activities for the folks who owned the place.

One of the entries I jotted down was, "One of these days, Missy is going to fall into that outhouse." Sure enough, "Mom, Mom!" I heard as Andy came running toward the cook shack, "Missy fell into the outhouse!" Fortunately, she hadn't fallen all the way through the hole in the seat which was a real blessing. All I could see of my scared little girl was two arms, the bottom of two feet and two big round eyes pleading for help. I tried not to laugh as I was pulling her out. To fall into that pit of poo would have been really traumatic. Mother's guilt hit immediately as I had encouraged her to go by herself. I always accompanied her after that.

Our time at Papa Bear was mostly quiet. We had pilot friends who would airdrop us ice cream, newspapers, cans of pop that exploded, and essential equipment. We made our needs known by CB radio. We had a lot of fun exploring the area. Beavers had built a dam across a tiny creek that entered the lake, we enjoyed watching them. We found a little sandy shore for a picnic one day. It was so hot (Yes, it does get hot in Alaska!) I let the kids take off their clothes and run through the stream and mud. We really had a good time that day.

I watched the incredible strength of my husband increase. The logs he used to build with were waterlogged; they had been cut down and sat absorbing rain for several years. They were big logs, fifteen to twenty feet long and one to two feet in diameter.

They were so heavy I couldn't even lift one end. I watched Don work with a steel cable overhead and a come-along winch maneuvering those monsters into place.

The logs went up in seven days. It was an incredible feat for one man. Don needed help when it was time to put on the large ridgepole, the highest log in the center of the ceiling that supports the roof. City girls aren't accustomed to precariously sitting on top of log buildings.

I've never been fond of heights and this was no exception! My job was to straddle a log that jutted out from the top of the wall, my feet dangling in the air. Don handed me a come-along pulley to winch back and forth, helping pull the top ridgepole into place. It sits on top of the gable ends on either side. It was too heavy for Don to push into place himself. I was supposed to assist with this. He said, "Okay, now on three. Are you ready?" I gulped and said, "Yeah, honey." Something went wrong with the come-along and I was trying frantically to make it work. I was listening to Don grunt and groan. He got it to the top but looked ready to pass out from the exertion. Just about that time the come-along clicked in and I started cranking on it saying, "Got it, I got it!" Don couldn't believe he had pushed that monstrous water-soared log on top by himself. I laughed about this little episode later. He didn't.

My folks came up to see us while we were there. Daddy flew his Super Cub on floats and my mom brought steaks! It was so good to see them. I begged my Dad to fly me back to Talkeetna but it was getting too late in the day. I was more than ready to go home, back to some running water and a hot bath. It was those amenities I missed the most. We were taking our baths in a little galvanized metal tub after hauling and heating the water. I was washing all the clothes by hand, hanging them out to dry then washing the kids in the same tub. Washing blue jeans by hand is a lot of work.

One of the hardest things to cope with in an Alaskan summer is the lack of darkness, especially while living in a tent. It was also hard to sleep at night because of the mosquitoes. All in all, it was an interesting experience in a beautiful unique place.

It took us ten years to move out of the basement and upstairs into our log home. I was so overwhelmed with the thought of sanding all those logs because I was allergic to sawdust. The ladies in my church planned a sanding day. They all brought lunch and worked all day, sanding the logs on the inside of the house! Then we applied log oil inside and out. We had wood floors, teal carpet, and a view of Christiansen Lake. Don had made a moose antler chandelier using four huge moose antlers that hung from the vaulted ceiling. It was beautiful! I could hear the soothing rain on the tin roof. It was so peaceful. It was comforting to know that all the water would run off the roof and not into my home! Quite sadly, Don and I separated that year and ended up divorcing. Don would go on to build another beautiful home on the lake and own a successful flying business.

GOLD MINING

1983 was a year to forget. We left that spring to gold mine. Our first project was building a two-story gold mining plant in Anchorage. We committed to gold mining all summer into the fall of that year. Don decided to take this job because our future was uncertain and we needed money. It didn't take much money to live but we didn't have any money left after the winter. Work was seasonal in Talkeetna; we saved through the summer to have enough for winter. We hoped for a prosperous summer with a promised bonus.

Gold miners arc very optimistic people. Don worked twelve to sixteen hours a day welding on the gold plant, a unit two stories high and longer than a long-haul trailer. This was simply an enlarged sluice-box that processed yards of soil at a time. When the crew got tired of welding, Don built a bazooka gun out of some pipe; they would light the bazooka and fire empty cans into the lot next door. As soon as the huge plant became operational, it was hauled over 300 miles from Anchorage to our first camp at Kantishna, outside the boundary of Mt. McKinley National Park (now called Denali National Park). We were all flown in knowing that Kantishna airstrip had a reputation as a place where many airplanes crashed on impact. Winds came up unexpectedly tossing small planes downwards and sideways. These are called wind shear conditions. People died on that airstrip. It was lined with crashed and abandoned planes. My kitchen window in our trailer overlooked the runway and I found myself praying for people's safety as the planes came and went. Although a dangerous airstrip, it was very busy.

Don worked midnight to noon driving a backhoe and running the plant. A large backhoe filled the plant with dirt, and gold was sorted from all the other debris as it came "sluicing" over a huge, shaking bed. Icy cold water was piped from the glacial creek and huge rock boulders were sorted out from the dirt. It was a tremendous thing. But it was a long haul for Don, he was always tired after a twelve-hour shift. The man worked seven days a week with no break. I had a baby to contend with so he could sleep.

Most mining camps are pretty rough places, but our boss really went out of his way to make it more pleasant for the women. We had a washer and dryer, and our single-wide trailer was very nice, but there wasn't much to do. We got a break one night and we went to a surveyor's camp down the road to watch a movie. There was no television and everything was run on a generator. A movie was a treat! I think that was our only night off the whole summer.

Our dog Boomer was big and full of energy by this time. We'd only been at mining camp for a few days when he disappeared. We were all enjoying a big feed at the boss's trailer before work started. Someone looked out the window and said, "Here comes the Parkey." A Denali National Park Ranger drove up and there sat Boomer like the guy's girlfriend, right next to him on the front seat. I went out to see where he'd gone and learned he ran five miles down the road just to say hello to everybody. Someone recognized him as part of our camp, and the nice ranger brought him back to us.

At the same moment everyone in the trailer started applauding, cheering and yelling at me to come back in. I had just missed our son's first steps, I now had a toddler on my hands. Whenever little Andy got restless I put him in my backpack, and we walked. It soothed him and got me outside. Imagine miles of mossy tundra divided by one dirt road on the edge of Mt. McKinley National Park. We see caribou, tourists, bears and more bears. Once, I was on my way back from a long walk when two men who mined upstream pulled along beside me and asked, "Did you know there's a bear a hundred yards behind you?" I looked at them and said, "Can you give us a lift?" I never saw the bear, but I took the ride back to camp just to be safe.

Andy grew and we walked, and he grew some more, and we walked. I finally got skinny. I found out I loved to ride motorcycles at mining camp. Don found an old one he fixed up for fun. I later bought a dirt bike of my own. To me, riding a dirt bike was like riding a horse and I left all my cares in the wind!

And Boomer, he was quite a dog. The survey crew had a helicopter pilot named Buddy who would fly crews in and out at all hours of the day and night. Word was spreading that he had seen a lone white wolf about twenty miles from camp. He was so excited about the sighting. He told everyone, "I saw it! I saw it!" About that time, I was wondering why Boomer never did anything but sleep all day. It was so unlike him. Each night I'd see him going under our trailer and in the morning he was still there. We soon discovered the identity of the mysterious "white wolf"—our dog. He had been running twenty miles into the hills every night! He ran back to get under our trailer before morning. He was incredible! Boomer never missed a walk with Andy and I no matter how tired he was. He was our protector. Buddy visited our camp once and realized it was Boomer he saw, not a wolf. Amazed, Buddy gazed at Boomer with admiration.

One-night Don went to work thirty minutes early and found a coworker Dave, who was trapped under a metal guard on the gold plants conveyor belt. He had been fed through up to his knees, with ice cold water and boulders falling on him for over thirty minutes. The only thing that had kept him from being totally fed between the metal guard and conveyor belt was that he was holding on to a bar above his head and resisting the pull on his lower body. He had been screaming over and over, but no one heard him above the roar of the machinery in the valley. Don was able to shut it down and extricate him from the machine. Thankfully, I had just completed Emergency Medical Training, so I knew how to help him. Kim, one of the other employees, had been a medic in the United States Air Force and I asked him to assist me on Dave's flight to the hospital. We had sheets and plywood to stabilize his wounds. Sleeping bags were put over him for warmth.

We loaded him into a small plane with the back four seats removed to make room for our injured friend.

We are taking off on a short airstrip, ending abruptly at a river. The fully loaded plane started rolling, and we rolled without catching air and I thought, *Something's terribly wrong; we have been on the ground way too long!* I bent my head and asked Jesus to help us. Out tires left the ground two inches short of going into the river and even grazed a tree climbing out. We made it!

Dave lost consciousness shortly after takeoff, succumbing to his plummeting blood pressure. He was in extreme shock. He was cold from ice water cascading onto him for over thirty minutes, and very pale. With no medical equipment, I asked Kim to raise the plywood board Dave was on so his lower extremities were higher than his head. This pushed oxygenated blood to his vital organs. I could faintly hear his breathing with my stethoscope. His beautiful blonde wife and Mother of their daughter was not prepared to see him die, she was so calm and brave. Soon Dave started responding to us again, such a relief! He eventually pulled through after undergoing surgery in Fairbanks. I was really thankful I'd had some medical training and knew what to do for him. The basics worked.

The gold plant was covered in blood the next day. Everyone was in shock and didn't work but they got the plant cleaned off. Dave lost much of his right calf and saphenous nerve that pulls up your foot when you walk. He had to wear a brace to walk but was thankful for it. Shortly after the accident Dave was back to work. He was minutes away from letting go and being fed entirely through that small space. They did revamp the gold plant and took that guard off the conveyor belt.

There were a handful of environmentalists that protested mining. Yes, the creek got stirred up and no the fish didn't die. When we left all the rocks were covered with top soil, growing grass. No person would know it had been mined. It was hard, dangerous work and most gold miners broke even financially if they were lucky. It was always a security concern. With all the gold miners on our creek, we would be on the lookout for strangers.

I had heard the term "gold fever" before, but I never understood what it meant until I witnessed it firsthand in the gold camps. When there was a cleanup of the gold plant, it was shut down and you could see the gold nuggets, hundreds of various sizes lying on top of the sifted soil. Sometimes we'd find thumb sized ones, sometimes little ones but always a lot of nuggets you could see with the naked eye. It was a mesmerizing sight. When cleanup time came it was interesting to see people's reactions.

If they had gold fever their eyes would glaze over and they would start to shake. Gold had a strange hold on them-like an addiction, like crack. Some folks couldn't get it out of their systems once they started mining for gold. Every year they would expect to strike it big, but it rarely happened.

That year there was a character named John Ski who worked in the mining camp. The boss sent him to carve a road forty miles long into the side of granite mountains. He worked for three weeks, alone on a bulldozer to accomplish it. It was an amazing feat. They moved most of the trailers and gold plant to Caribou Creek. When they were moving that huge plant to a higher spot in the mountains, it started to fall off the road. Buddy the pilot happened to be flying over in his helicopter exactly at that critical moment. He latched onto the top of the plant from above, pulling it back onto the road as the crew drove forward. It was an 1,800 foot drop to the valley below. That move to Caribou Camp was a wild and hair-raising trip. The families were flown in, hurtling onto a short mud covered airstrip. It was terrifying, but once again we survived!

We got settled in a tiny fifteen-foot travel trailer which had a huge hole in the door that had been covered with a plywood board. I was told a grizzly bear tried to break into the trailer and eat the last occupant. The man shot the bear through the door in defense and killed it. That was encouraging! Our only lighting source was kerosene lamps, so the trailer was dark. And it was grimy, the kind of grime you couldn't scrub clean. In the subfreezing temperatures pipes froze and broke. Water poured onto our floor three inches deep one morning and we lived with a wet floor from then on. Every morning our boots would be frozen to the floor and had to be pried loose. It was necessary to keep little Andy up off the floor the entire time—a hard thing to do with an active toddler just learning to walk. One of my treasured pictures is of our son getting a bath in my big stainless steel bread bowl with a huge grin on his face. He was a happy baby.

There was three inches of snow on the ground. We lived in a small valley surrounded by tall mountains and freezing weather. It was miserable outside and hard on the workers.

One nice day at Caribou Creek, several of us were out walking and my friend Shirley said, "Look at that!" We all looked up toward the mountains and there was a caribou, running across the mountainside as fast as it could with its tongue hanging out, Boomer right behind it, closing fast. He must have been running thirty miles an hour—he was shooting across that mountain. That dog loved mining camp! Unlike Boomer, I couldn't wait to get out of Caribou Creek. Don had to stay at the mining camp and keep working until everything totally froze up.

Andy and I flew out only to be weathered in at Nenana, halfway home to Talkeetna. We ended up in a trailer hotel there—the only one in town—and I couldn't wait for a hot bath and some sleep. As I opened the door to our hotel room holding my baby Andy, I noticed two small holes in the wall about eye height. I thought, *That's odd!* I looked down to see the huge round dried bloodstain on the floor. That answered the question about where the two holes came from! So there I was in the room where someone had been shot, with my little baby. I got my bags, baggage, and crib for Andy settled. Andy fell quietly asleep and I went into the bathroom to take the nice long hot bath. There was no hot water! Reluctantly I skipped my bath, (It had only been a month). Shoving toilet paper into the bullet holes for privacy, I went to bed. I had taken everything but our kitchen sinks up to the mining camp and I had brought about that much back. As it turned out everybody who had flown out of camp came over and helped me move to the train and get me aboard. It was a beautiful ride home on the train. Andy ran up and down the aisle and made people smile. We watched the scenery that was gloriously green!

I had left a freezing, snow-covered mining camp to find the rest of the world was still in late summer! When I arrived back in Talkeetna, the first thing I saw was signs that said, "Welcome Home, Nancy." There stood a little group of well-wishers, including my brother and sister-in-law, their kids, Don's sister Susan, and old friends, all welcoming me home. I was so happy to be there, tears just flowed from my eyes. I couldn't hold them back. Then I experienced a kind of climate shock because when I left mining camp it was the month of October, and already snow and darkness ruled. Talkeetna was still warm, sunny and green, I thought it had to be July! I was so glad to be back; I was laughing, crying, and hugging everybody. People thought I was crazy! I thought I was crazy! I probably was!

ANIMALS OF ALASKA

Dogs and Cats

You can't live in Alaska without being surrounded by animals of all kinds—both wild and domestic. Dog sledding is popular in Alaska and dog sledding stories abound. I have a story about my good friend Susan telling how difficult it is to drive a dog sled team. Susan is an independent, very rugged Minnesota girl, bound and determined to learn how to run sled dogs. She wanted to surprise her husband Jeff because that's what he did to earn a living as a guide in winter.

One day she took a full team of eight excited dogs out for a run. Usually you start with two dogs and add to the string slowly. She didn't want the dogs to get away from her, so she tied a rope around her ankle to the sled. The dogs took off like a slingshot out the driveway without her even giving them the signal, catching her off guard. Now upended, Susan was dragged on her back behind the sled screaming at the top of her lungs! Luckily, her neighbor Dave Parker heard her screams and jumped onto the sled getting the situation under control. He saved her life. Despite the scare, this activity meant so much to her she kept trying.

That same winter my husband Don happened to drive up the road toward her house, meeting her dog team running full out. Susan hadn't tied herself to the sled this time but the dogs took off and got away from her. She had managed to leap into the sled and there she was terrified, riding along completely out of control. The dogs would not stop. This could have been a horrible accident with the dogs running in front of a car, chasing a moose or another dog sled team. Don jumped on the back runners as the team passed him braking until they stopped, saving her again. She was so determined. Another time her dogs just flat got away—without her. Somebody had to go up in an airplane and spot them from the air. They were hung up on a tree miles away but eventually retrieved safely. The good news is her persistence paid off; she didn't quit and successfully learned to command her dog team. Every woman I know who runs dog teams is eventually bruised and has suffered broken bones. It's really a rough sport for men and women to engage in.

However, men have a different touch with the dogs. Dogs are kind of like kids—when the man speaks, they obey! A fellow in Talkeetna by the name of Pecos had a beautiful dog team. He would take them out in fields and give them commands that the human ear can't hear and his lead dog would do whatever he asked. He ran them through a series of figure eights and various paces which never ceased to amaze me. I'd take a horse with reins any day, but I sure wouldn't trust a team of dogs.

Our golden retriever Boomer, used to pull us. After being tied up all day he would be bursting with energy. When we lived out at our first cabin, I hauled water from our neighbors. They lived about a quarter of a mile from us. I got a little plastic sled out and with a harness attached it to Boomer, put in my five-gallon water jug, sat down on the jug and yell, "Go, Boomer!" Off we'd fly. He took me over there okay but he'd never bring me back. (I think he just didn't want to go home!) I had to get out and lead him back with a full water jug in the sled, but that's how I got water all that winter. Neighbors are truly lifesavers in Alaska, providing fun, fellowship, and survival.

Some friends borrowed a snow machine from us one cold winter's day. They had property a long way up the railroad tracks and used our big heavy duty Alpine snow machine. Naturally, the thing broke down and they came back without it. Don had to retrieve it before dark through deep snow and intense cold. He put his toolbox and extra gas in a plastic sled and left dragging the sled, with Boomer bounding along beside him. Don soon tired, hooking Boomer to the sled Don sat on the toolbox. Boomer pulled him the rest of the three miles up the railroad tracks. He discovered the snow machine was out of gas, he refueled it and made it back to the cabin. Boomer earned a look of admiration from his owner while Don told the story.

Cats are a great pet to have where mice invade cabins. When we lived in that first cabin we had an orange kitten that would stand or lie down under our barrel stove for warmth every morning. He lived there most of the time with only a half-inch between his fur and the stove, he loved it. The problem was that Boomer loved the cat and wanted to play with him. We were eating dinner one night and we smelled something awful, like something burning. Boomer had been over by the stove trying to entice that cat into playing with him. We called him over discovering half of his side was burned black from being too close to the stove. That cat Missy Boots was never charred from the stove but Boomer's hair was constantly singed. (A lot of my polyester pants also fell victim to that stove when I got too close on Sunday mornings trying to get warm!)

Moose

When I was three years old, I developed a staph infection in my left wrist bone and wound up critically ill in the hospital. I remember my strong Father carrying me into the hospital, all bundled up in a blanket and the shots in my fanny. They wheeled me into the operating room where no one spoke and Mom stood watching from the doorway. A mask was put over my face and I screamed. I was in the hospital three weeks and barely lived. I owe my life at that time to Dr. Bill Mills and Dr. John Tower. Together they operated, cleaned out the infection and miraculously picked the right antibiotics to fight the infection. Antibiotics were a new medical development and this type of infection was rare in children. My hair went from super curly to straight due to the illness and medications administered.

While in the hospital one of my memories was looking into the room across the hall from me, where a boy who looked older than me sat up in bed. He was suffering from injuries due to the most perfect hoof print on his forehead, the perfect hoof print of a moose! I heard later that the moose had wandered downtown where people yelled at the animal and car horns honked to scare the moose away. In desperation the animal ran right over the kid in the next room and left his print behind! He recovered but was seriously stomped!

When we lived in the city before the earthquake it was a common occurrence to see a frightened moose running down the street, looking for a way to escape. Often the moose would be entangled in a child's metal swing set or a clothes line.

They're funny creatures—my Mother would say they are so ugly they're cute! The old ones are larger than a horse and capable of demolishing cars when hit on the road. The increasing population in

Alaska presents problems for moose with more vehicles on the highways and roads. Winter finds them walking on plowed railroad tracks. Our Alaska Railroad kills them only when they jump in front of the train and it cannot stop. The snow (twenty-two feet one year) makes it impossible for them to get off the highways also. The moose suffered from lack of food due to the tremendous snowfall of 1991. The snow had covered treetops and houses. Severe cold temperatures fell to forty and fifty below zero leaving the moose starving to death and dropping in their tracks. Makes one wonder how the moose population can be sustained with so many deaths. The Alaska Department of Fish and Game does an excellent job regulating the states wild animal and fish populations. On one trip to Wasilla from Talkeetna after the record snowfall, I counted thirteen live moose! I was thankful that the big creatures had rebounded from that difficult winter.

As a child I often watched moose in my parent's backyard and pasture eating our decorative trees in the yard. My Dad would get his BB gun out. I'm certain they ran more from the noise than the BBs hitting their thick brown coats. The door would slam, the dogs ran out barking, Dad would be yelling at the dogs and the slight sound of the BB gun was drowned in the ruckus. My horses and moose got along fine. I think they respectfully left each other alone. From my experience wild animals will usually take the path of least resistance, retreating rather than attacking.

My favorite moose story involves a mommy and her twins that took up residence in my parents' back pasture after my horse left. We first noticed the mama moose while enjoying a barbecue on my parents' deck. We were celebrating their fiftieth wedding anniversary when the moose wandered right up to the railing on the deck, ten feet from us. My cousin Bill commented that perhaps a dog had attacked the poor thing because she had blood on her back legs. As we turned toward her, two wet and wobbly newborn baby moose appeared and she allowed them to come close like she was putting them on display. Each spring over the next five years she bore twins and as soon as they could walk, she ushered them under my parents' dining room window to show them off and to say thank you for her lovely home in our pasture. When she finally had to move on to other forage, we missed her and all her little ones. Unbelievably years later I was talking to a medical office manager I worked with in Grand Junction, Colorado, and she knew the moose! It turned out that her brother lived one street over from my parents in Anchorage. The same mama moose visited their house too! She did the same thing, bringing her babies by for all to admire. What an amazing coincidence!

Moose often become accustomed to humans and grow fairly tame over time. Once while Mom was working at the kitchen sink she sensed that something was watching her. She turned and met the eyes of a huge moose looking at her through the front window! To find that perch it had to climb an icy rock staircase. Another time a moose with a wide horn rack stood in the same place looking into our living room inches from glass picture windows. Mom said to stand perfectly still, thank goodness it didn't come through or break the windows! Moose are regular peeping toms!

Once I was watching a moose gazing through our tall pasture gate. From a standstill, the animal soared over the gate with very little effort.

In May of 1989, an historic event happened which surprised us all—our Mother finally gave up her garden. It had been her pride and joy since we moved there after the earthquake, and she was sad to have to call it quits. She had decided it was growing more for the moose family than for our family. My parents ordered sod to cover it, knowing the moose were really going to be disappointed with no more lettuce, broccoli, cauliflower, turnips and carrots to munch on throughout the summer. Mother had fed them well for many years.

Caribou

While flying we headed up a valley with mountains on either side. The land in between the mountains was filled with hundreds of Caribou. It was a sea of moving antlers and animals packed tightly together into the large flat valley. The name caribou is interchangeable with the name reindeer because they are so similar, the animals are cousins. Some old-timers remember standing among herds of thousands.

Musk Ox

This is a type of short legged cloven-hoofed hairy beast with water buffalo horns. The fur coat they grow is highly sought after by weavers and knitters. The overcoat of hair they grow is two to three feet in length with a thick soft wool undercoat. The herds gather far north. I did see some at the Alaska Zoo. I highly recommend the Alaska Zoo in Anchorage for its variety of Alaskan animals, and some not Alaskan. I have been there many times and have not been disappointed.

Seals, Sea Lions, and Orcas

The wildlife in Alaska is second to none, and one of the most exciting aspects of the state. My favorite place to visit is Homer, Alaska, where a huge spit of land juts out 4.5 miles into Kachemak Bay. It has both a port and a deep-water port for the large ships. It serves 1500 ships a year. It was damaged in the 1964 earthquake by a tsunami but repaired afterward. On this spit is the dock for a small charter boat named the *Danny J*, which takes visitors across Katchemak Bay to a small cove called Halibut Cove. My sister-in-law Roni and I went ocean kayaking there one day and had quite an adventure.

We took our kayaks on board the *Danny J* and sailed past a rookery, lingering to watch the birds come and go. The rookery had all kinds of birds, including puffins, one of my favorites. They eat so much fish they cannot fly and can only float on top of the water. Once the food is digested they are light enough to crawl up on a safe rock again.

Halibut Cove was once a tiny community that has now been turned into art shops. It has also become a harbor seal refuge for orphaned baby seals that are so cute! Their big round eyes just pull you into loving them. Some need to be bottle fed, a total labor of love for those volunteers. Once the seals grow large enough they are released back into the wild. We stopped a short while to watch the orphaned baby seals playing there. They were curious about the kayaks and came along side to visit us. It was pure joy.

We tore ourselves away to paddle out into the ocean along the border of the island. Roni was hugging the coast not willing to venture too far out. We went under a massive rock arch that surprised us, we didn't know it was there. I saw an orca (killer whale) breech about 300 yards from me and I was immediately ready to go explore the whole ocean! Then there appeared a 500-pound steller sea lion on my right side. It just popped up like a cork about two feet from my kayak—I could have reached out and touched its head! Behind me were two others, one a huge male weighing at least 700 pounds. I was in heaven with glee, but Roni was intelligently leery of the massive beasts and kept warning me with a low voice to get closer to shore. Soon the other two came up to my boat and were checking me out, I was lost in the experience and talking to them as they hungrily eyed me.

The trio eventually departed, we went innocently on our way. Back aboard the *Danny J* I struck up a conversation with the lady skipper, she told me that the Steller sea lions travel in packs of three and attack kayakers! Roni and I looked at each other—silence. We knew someone had been watching over us. I was spared again while being in the presence of imposing creatures.

I did grow up with a hair seal named Oley. I learned to ride and jump horses at Diamond H Ranch. They had an indoor riding arena for winter riding. Mr. Oley the seal made riding in the arena a scary thing for the horses. His pool was in one corner of the arena and I believe Oley would wait for a horse to approach, then scare them with exploding splashes in his pool. Sammye Seawell, the owner with her husband Howard, was an avid animal lover and had taken this abandoned hair seal baby in. For some reason he was not released back into the wild and grew up at the ranch. Hair seals now are endangered and Sammye would take Oley to elementary schools during educational teaching with him. Oley was a star. He would propel himself in a modified worm motion or be pulled into class by a red wagon. Not being a land animal his grace was reserved for the water. Most horses got used to him. He was an unexpected character to have around.

Bears

Everyone has heard of Alaskan bears and seen pictures of their antics. Comical and terrifying at the same time, they are a large looming presence in spring, summer, and fall. No matter where you go in Alaska, bears are there. Perhaps the most famous Alaskan bear was Binky the

Polar Bear. He came to the Alaskan Zoo as an orphan and grew to be a popular attraction. He got famous for trying to eat a tourist that got too close to his cage. He instantly reached through the cage bars and got the lady's thigh in his mouth. She ended up keeping her leg and Binky kept her shoe as a trophy, parading around with it in his mouth for several days.

Six months pregnant with our first child, I flew down the Alaska Peninsula to Cold Bay with Don. We met a friend in Cold Bay who wanted to bear hunt. The bear's habitat in this region is treeless, savage and raw, a visual feast to fly over. On the way down, I was throwing up every twenty minutes with air sickness just like I did at the age of twelve. Being pregnant was bad enough but being in an airplane compounded my misery.

During the flight Don would call out, "Look at the whale! Look, whales!" I'd turn to the window and see two eighty-foot humpback whales in crystal clear turquoise ocean water. I couldn't stand to miss the view and couldn't stand to watch it go by as the motion sickness would erupt again. I saw a proud walrus surveying his ocean home from a rock throne high above the ocean. Don landed the Super Cub on a black sand beach and we collected armfuls of old glass Japanese fishing floats still tied in rope worn by salt water. Then off we'd go again and off would go my stomach!

At one point we had to stop for the night at the airport in King Salmon. A frigid blowing wind met us as we parked the plane. We had no place to go so an empty airport luggage container served as our room that night. We threw our sleeping bags down inside, and there we slept. Not exactly the Hilton, but it sufficed.

Once we arrived at Cold Bay I was totally enchanted. Cold Bay has a reputation for hostile weather but it was sunny and clear while I visited. It was fall, the mountains were in full color—reds and oranges. The first night after setting up camp, the men left. I was alone in the most rugged country you can imagine. This was *Big Bear* country, and I mean *huge*! Years earlier Don had guided in this area and helped shoot a bear that was a world record. These are the most beautiful animals. Hunting regulations stipulated that the two men could not fly an airplane and shoot an animal the same day. Don and the friend needed to find a spot to camp that night. The high powered rifles went with the hunters and I was left to defend myself with a .22 pistol. (The bear would have seen that tiny gun and probably died laughing!)

Cold Bay could have a five-star resort and many visitors if it was warm. I woke to a warm sunny day after a fitful night's sleep. The weather there is usually wind at 40-70 miles per hour that forcefully blows sand. The next day was again unusually sunny and relatively warm. The ocean was on the other side of a small hill and I had to explore. I found a tide pool in black volcanic rock full of tiny crabs. This captured my attention the whole morning. I walked to the top of a hill overlooking the ocean and soaked up the sun. Ocean in Anchorage is Cook Inlet, named after the famous explorer Captain Cook. It has the second highest tides in the world constantly stirring up glacial silt and mud. The inlet silt causes it to be a silky gray color throughout, not the blue of an ocean. Clear ocean fascinates me. A noise unlike any other I have ever heard grabbed me out of my sunbath. It was the spout of a mature Humpback Whale! It glided effortlessly twenty feet from me until at last I witnessed the tail fluke. It was magic!

Walking back to my camp, I was a little nervous about bears showing up since I would be cooking. I spent a beautiful night alone, looking for silhouettes of bears on the horizon. I spied two dark forms in a meadow three-quarters of a mile away. Watching them for the better part of an hour, I could swear they were moving, getting closer! I pondered what I would do against a bear that size, here were two of them! I finally decided the bears were only tree stumps, just two stumps in the middle of a field. Things do move if stared at long enough. I went to sleep telling myself everything would be all right, and it was. I was relieved that no bears were shot on this trip but some were seen. Looking for a camp spot our first day, we landed on a lake and spotted a magnificent bear on the other side. He paused looking straight at us and it seemed to me with sad heavy steps he continued on. He knew he was being hunted.

Another tale on my friend Susan: she decided to go camping in the Talkeetna wilderness overnight with no weapon, pepper spray or radio. She took her sleeping bag, tent and some food. I had cautioned her about going out alone and unarmed. Off she went, alone and unarmed. The next day she came back enormously traumatized and told the story of what befell her. It seems she made it to her campsite, set up the tent, settling in for the night. Two grizzly cubs came along in the early morning and started batting at the tent, one on either side, while Susan screamed and prayed. The Mother had to be close by, and the thought paralyzed Susan with fear. She didn't know whether to run or stay put. Miraculously the cubs stopped the onslaught, the Mother did not show up, and the cubs finally ran off searching for more adventure. This turned out well, but there are many bear encounters that do not.

    My Father competed in triathlons with his good friends George Etsel and Marcie Trent, all were grandparents. Dad swam, George biked, and Marcie ran, they were a team for many years. Marcie unexpectedly was killed by a bear while running up a popular hiking trail. She had gone with her son and grandson to run McHugh Creek. This dense wooded area is outside of Anchorage toward Mt. Alyeska. A bear had killed a moose just off the trail. They ran up the trail past the kill, the bear came out and killed Marcie with one swipe of its paw and killed her son with another. Her grandson lived by climbing up a tree until help came. It was tragic. I watched for Beluga whales in Cook Inlet from the top of this trail and climbed it alone often.

AIRPLANES

You can't live in Alaska for very long without gathering some unusual, funny, or terrifying airplane stories. I didn't really like planes until I was about fifteen, because I would throw up every time I flew in one from motion sickness. It was the main mode of transportation in wild Alaska—many flew out of necessity. Alaska has so few roads and highways, planes were a great way to travel throughout the state. Lake Hood in Anchorage is the largest float plane base in the world. Due to the numerous lakes in Alaska many planes in the summer months are equipped with small pontoon-like metal floats instead of wheels. People like the late John Denver (he came to visit Talkeetna and had a great sing with musicians at the Fairview Inn, a local bar) had float planes that could also land on a runway. This works great until you takeoff from a runway and land on a lake. Forgetting to bring up your wheels, they drag on the water and cause the plane to flip over.

Don and I awoke one morning to find our neighbor's float plane upside down in the lake. We needed to see if everything was okay, I refused to go. Don boated out to the aircraft and examined it. When our friend flipped, he was so full of adrenaline that he kicked the thick plastic front window out. That is extremely difficult. But he survived.

The famous test pilot Brigadier General Chuck Yeager visited Anchorage once and commented that people use light planes here like Nebraskans use pickup trucks! My Father was a news item in the Anchorage Daily News when he made an emergency landing with his Super Cub. He was on approach to the runway at Anchorage International Airport when he looked down and saw his left tire coming off. He called the tower and they had him go around the pattern a few times to get rid of fuel while emergency services got to the runway. As Dad approached, he held the plane onto the right tire and when it came down on the left tire it fell off, the plane did a small loop and gently stopped. He got out to applause.

At sixteen I was hungry to learn to fly. When I announced to my dad that I wanted to take flying lessons, he said, "Oh, I'll take you flying." I was anxious but eager to learn. Once we got in the air, I had a whole different perspective from the back seat! You can't see the instruments! Super Cubs are flown with a stick and not a yoke or steering wheel. Dad, not being an instructor hadn't bothered to explain to me what everything did. No matter what, I could not get that plane to do what I wanted it to do which scared me to death. After about ten minutes I said, "I want you to fly Dad."

He took over the controls and said, "On the way home, we'll do some stalls." To me a "stall" meant the engine would quit. The plane would spin into the ground and you died. Ignorance was not bliss. I sat back in my seat white-knuckled and ready to throw up. "Doing stalls" was not fun at all. If you're going to learn to fly take my advice—go with a certified instructor not a well-meaning relative or friend. That was the end of my desire to be a pilot for a while.

The flying bug came back when I lived in Talkeetna, the village where mountain climbers fly to Mt. McKinley (or Denali which is the original Indian name of the mountain meaning "Great One"). Planes were always overhead. I started lessons in a small two seat Cessna 150 and soloed after ten hours of instruction.

My first flight with Don was very interesting. It was also our first date. Since he was apparently afraid to ask me, I had invited myself to go along. He was going to Stephan Lake. He put me in the front seat of his Super Cub because I was taking flying lessons. I wanted to try my hand at flying the Super Cub which is a tail dragger. A tail dragger has a third wheel on the end of the airplane tail where a Cessna 150 has a tripod based set of wheels. Everything was foreign. A tail dragger can be very tricky to fly because the wind can flip the plane over or from side to side easily. Don crawled in the back and as we were taking off down the village airstrip, we had a power loss after hearing a "pop." Don was immediately on the radio, "Emergency! Emergency! Mayday! Mayday!" Taking the controls, he swung the plane onto the maintained state airstrip.

This was not a promising start. I got out and watched him fly around for a while, testing the plane. He landed saying everything seemed fine, so away we went with Don in the pilot seat. Turned out that the manifold had collapsed, a serious malfunction. We were flying in Don's Cub the second time with me in the front and he said, "Let's take it out and do some stalls." I had learned that stalls weren't difficult—you just lost a little bit of air under the wings, and the plane gently dipped until power was applied. The engine didn't quit and you did not spin into the ground.

Logic had overcome my vivid childhood imaginations. I was adept at doing stalls in my rented Cessna 150. Don failed to tell me, however, that he was going to have me pull the Super Cub stick back and set the baby up on its tail. The plane is totally perpendicular to the rest of the world before it'll stall, or so I was told. So there we were at 2,000 feet, practicing stalls. I pulled back on the stick, and I pulled back on the stick, until we were looking right up at the sky much like being on a shuttle launch. The tail failed to ascend and slipped toward the earth. Screaming, I let go of the stick. The nose dropped sending the plane into a spin. Don was able to recover it. He was a little miffed at me. He couldn't believe I did that, and I couldn't believe that he didn't explain to me that Super Cubs don't stall gently like Cessna 150s.

I think I've done most of my praying in airplanes or about airplanes. Many things can happen during flight and you cannot pull over to the side and stop. You figure it out. The following incident is a good illustration of why I prayed so much in planes.

It was a beautiful day for a flight. Don, Boomer and I took a commercial Cessna 180 airplane to Anchorage for an annual mechanical checkup. After a few minutes the mechanic said, "Come here. I want to show you something." He opened up the back cargo door and showed us the elevator cable, which makes the plane go up and down. If the cable had broken the plane would have plummeted into the ground. It normally consists of seven metal strands; this cable was frayed and held by one delicate strand. The mechanic said, "It's a miracle it didn't let go! One more takeoff and you would have been dead." Silence. That's why I prayed a lot, but I would never have given up flying. It's so wonderful to let go of this earth, putting your life into perspective and clearing your mind. Everything is so peaceful. There is nothing like the serenity of being alone in an airplane at sunset. I was reminded of Alaska's beauty every time I got in the air.

Airplane crashes are a part of life on the Last Frontier. Don Sheldon, a famous bush pilot was thought to have crashed thirty-two planes. Amazingly no person was killed. Don lost a lot of planes but he was a local hero for all his flying. Cliff Hudson, a steady, quiet man, also a famous bush pilot, was known to have never had one accident. Bad things in Alaska can happen fast. With so many planes in use, crashes are a part of life in Alaska.

I finally got my private pilot license after having my son Andy. A gal that worked in the flight service station named Corky, took lessons after me. She spun the same little Cessna 150 that I had gotten my pilot's license in into the ground, upside down in a subdivision, and walked away!

I had Doug Geeting for a flight instructor, he was also an acrobatic pilot. He taught me well, but it didn't keep me from getting in a near midair collision. I was practicing touch-and-go's one afternoon. A touch and go is a landing that you simply touch down and immediately take off again. I could neither see or hear any other plane coming into the flight pattern. Every airport has a local frequency for the Flight Service Station. Pilots can broadcast their position so other planes in the area are aware. I had done several takeoffs and landings. I had corrected my altitude fifty feet higher on the downwind approach and did another touch-and-go. I saw an airplane stopped on the runway which was unusual. I didn't know how the commuter plane had landed there. I found out later that as they dropped down into the flight pattern, I was gaining altitude and appeared in front of them with inches to spare. We had not seen each other. The pilot was so shook up they landed behind me and came to a full stop on the runway. That was the closest call I had.

One hunting season a dear friend flipped a Helio Courier landing on a short dirt runway. The Helio is a high-performance six-passenger plane. He had clients in many hunting camps positioned all over the Talkeetna Mountains. Don hopped in the Super Cub to help him, bringing him home for supper. The fellow had been awake for two days and nights working on his plane. By the time he got to our house, he was exhausted. We ate dinner and he was asleep before his head hit the pillow on our living room rollaway. He must have begun snoring as our dog Boomer, pointed his nose to the heavens, started howling a foot away from his head. Our friend was so dead to the world, the noise didn't even cause him to stir. Don helped him retrieve his hunters and everything was fine. When things like this happen you need a person like Don who knows the area well enough to find hunting camps without a map. A description of the area is all a pilot would have to go on. It is a vast place. Hunting guides have their own secret places for camps. The thing that got me through stressful times was my faith.

One morning Don was out flying and I was praying for him as usual. As I did a picture of a little metal strip just popped into my mind. It was just a thin metal strip, so I prayed for God to strengthen it and any screws and bolts and anything around it. I asked God to set angels on the wings of Don's airplane. I asked for his protection then forgot about it. When Don came home that evening, he sat down looking more serious than I had ever seen him. He asked, "Did you pray for me today?" I said I had. He said, "What did you pray for?" I'd momentarily forgotten all the specifics of that morning prayer so I said, "I prayed for your protection." And then the story came out. After he had landed, he discovered that the plane's wheel strut had come loose and only being held to the plane by one thin metal strip. If that had come off, or if he had not made a perfect landing, he would have been dead. The plane would have rolled up in a ball. That gave me the courage I needed for Don's flying years.

Before I met Don, he went on a search and rescue mission only to be rescued himself! Don was working at Stephan Lake Lodge when a friend, Jim Sharpe picked him up to go on a search and rescue mission, Don jumped in the Super Cub still in his hip boots. After flying until fuel was low they decided to look up one more canyon. They spotted the crashed plane with no survivors. Just as they radioed in the crash location, their own plane stalled and crashed. In the initial crash the passenger in the back seat had been impaled by the wing strut, which passed completely through his body. When Don came to after the accident, he found himself outside the plane on his knees with no idea how he got free of his seatbelt and out of the plane. As in the other accident, the wing strut had gone through the back seat. Had he still been sitting there he would have been killed instantly. Both he and Jim Sharpe ended up with broken backs as well as other less serious injuries. There were three miracles that day. The first was that Don got out of the back seat somehow. The second miracle was that no fire ignited, even though the Super Cub's battery had sparked, arcing into the gas tank upon impact. The third miracle was that a military helicopter responding to their radio call arrived within minutes. The soldiers jumped out with body bags, only to discover they had live people to rescue.

Airplane stories cannot be told without sharing the loss of close friends and family. Healing is sought in the telling of the story and this is my story.

To this day I don't remember the date it happened—I barely remember the year. It must have been 1982 because I was heavily pregnant with Andy. Don and I were sitting on our couch drinking a cup of tea one Sunday afternoon. My brother Jim came over and told us sad news that our brother John and his wife Deena, who was six months pregnant, were in a plane crash. It was unknown if anyone was alive. They were aboard a plane that had gone down and rescuers were attempting to reach the site but weather was not permitting it. I'd lost several acquaintances, but this was the first time I had possibly lost anyone so close to me. It was so hard to believe. John and his friends, Clark and Melinda Gruening, had been developing a fishing resort in Warm Springs Bay outside of Sitka, Alaska. John was so excited about it. It's a beautiful deep bay where you can see killer whales and catch large halibut. Mom and Dad had just returned from visiting John and Deena and had a wonderful time. John always had a terrible fear of flying. He wouldn't even fly up to Mt. McKinley with the family.

One day he looked at me and said, "You know, Nancy, I just can't put my whole family on a plane."' He was always very spiritually sensitive and I think he knew his fate. When we were young my Mother and Father never flew in the same commercial plane because of the possibility of an accident. Alaskan aviation is risky. Small planes in Alaska are at the highest risk. My oldest brother John hated airplanes, even big ones.

For some reason instead of taking a boat that day, John and Deena chose to fly. They flew in a six-seater plane on floats; along with the pilot and one other passenger. My big strong thirty-three-year-old brother John and beautiful six-month pregnant wife Deena in the back. Crossing a mountain pass they hit clear air turbulence, the FAA report stated something like this, "It was as though a giant hand took the plane, turned it upside down, and smashed it to the earth." Upside down they were thrown to the mountain side killing everyone instantly. High adventure carries a high cost. A rescue team finally arrived on the accident site and found no survivors. We were in shock, all of us. There was now no hope, they were gone. We were all sitting in Mom and Dad's living room crying, with Scott Hayworth, one of Johns closest friends. Crystal. my two-year-old niece, took a Kleenex box and started passing out one Kleenex to each person. We all laughed at her act of love and concern, breaking the heaviness of the situation for a moment.

Deena was of Greek heritage, having long dark hair and luminous blue eyes—a goddess to me inside and out. I admired her so much; she was always happy, loved people and people loved her. She and John were best friends in life. They were amazing partners. Once they were kayaking with another couple and camped overnight on a small beach across from a glacier. The glacier "calved" off a 200-foot chunk of ice creating a fatal tidal wave. The four friends were trapped against a rock wall, and knew they were going to die as they watched the wave approach. John's friend asked him if he was afraid to die, and John replied, "I'm not afraid to die with the woman I love." The threatening wave dissipated for reasons unknown, they were safe.

The months that followed the accident were trying, but the peace of God in our hearts brought us so much comfort, knowing they were in heaven with the Lord Jesus Christ. A quadriplegic lady living in Oregon, called Deena's Grandmother one day, "I have something I don't understand but I've got to tell you." She continued, "I keep seeing a vision of Deena. She's dressed in a long white robe, and she looks beautiful. She keeps coming to me and saying, "Tell Grandma, tell Grandma that it's beautiful here. It's just like Alaska!' Behind her, stood a man and a little boy." She hadn't known Deena very well, and she wasn't aware that Deena had been pregnant. I think it was the Lord's way of giving us comfort. The accident was hardest on my Dad as he saw the crushed bodies, saying the head injuries were so severe he could hardly tell who they were. For a year he continued to be so sad. Then one time when we were visiting he seemed to be his old self. He was lighter, not carrying the weight of losing a son and daughter so vital and full of life. When we were alone I asked him what had changed? He paused, very quietly telling me he had seen John and Deena. They had appeared to him as he was walking up the driveway bringing back the mail. He said, "John and Deena were standing there on the grass just like they were alive. I think it was to let me know they were okay. I told them, 'I love you kids' then they disappeared." I believe he had a visitation that lifted him out of the despair of losing them. They were fine, and he was too.

TROUBLE ON THE MOUNTAIN

December of 1981, a friend of ours crashed his Cessna 185 airplane on Mt. McKinley. It was one of the worst crashes I can remember because the very serious rescue was hindered by bad weather, and no one could reach them. This is how I remember it happening.

As I remember, my good friend, pilot Ed Hommer had taken his brother-in-law and two friends sightseeing around the mountain. It was winter and ten below zero—a sharply clear pristine day. Crossing above Kahiltna Pass they hit clear air turbulence. Clear air turbulence cannot be seen, there is no warning for it and every mountain pilot fears it. A terrific downdraft struck the plane smashing it violently onto Kahiltna Pass at 10,320 foot elevation. All on board were unconscious. The two men in the back seats took the hardest impact of the accident leaving them fatally injured with multiple fractures and internal bleeding. Dusk was falling when a Military C-130 picked up an ELT (Emergency Locater Transmitter) signal on the mountain. Doug Geeting ran to his Super Cub flying directly to the wreckage. Ed Hommer had found a flashlight and was signaling, landing lights flashed back! Rescue should be tomorrow; a group of local climbers were assembling as darkness fell on the survivors. During the night, Ed's brother-in-law Dan died of his injuries. The others were exposed to a wind chill of fifty degrees below zero. A few candy bars they had brought along was the only food. They wore warm clothes and boots, but not sufficient for that kind of biting cold and violent wind. The following morning Talkeetna Air Taxi pilots were in the air. Doug Geeting and Don flew over the pass dropping survival equipment, camp stoves, food, water, and sleeping bags while Lowell Thomas Jr., flew cover above. Most supplies slid down the steep 2,000-foot slope before the men could catch them. The plane came loose that afternoon, careening down the slope with their companion inside, stopping miraculously before dropping thousands of feet. The severely injured man was stretched out in the fuselage and now was hopelessly tangled in the wreckage. He died that night. In his grief Ed somehow kicked off his bunny boots and froze both his feet. His other friend was getting severe frostbite on his extremities.

Each flyby they did was harrowing due to the continuing severe clear air turbulence over the pass, which would cause the planes to drop and twist violently each time. An Army CH-47 Chinook helicopter was dispatched for rescue with a local group of climbers on board but it was buffeted so badly by winds that it could not land safely. The rescue crew, made up of volunteer local climbers, got in day four and started their climb to reach the plane. They started from the base camp on Kahiltna glacier at 5,000 feet and climbed up and over Kahiltna Pass to bring the two survivors back to base camp for pick up. Ed and his friend had frostbite so badly they had to ride in sleds and be pulled. All of the rescue team were friends with Ed and his wife Sandy. They got their friends rescued because of sheer determination and perseverance.

Mt. McKinley can stay clouded over for weeks, this was the worst possible time for it to go into hiding. The mountain weather can change in five minutes from a beautiful sunny day to clouds with sleet and snow—it's unforgiving. Due to the horrendous winds slamming the pass and whiteout conditions, it was five days before the plane crash survivors were rescued off the mountain. Two of the four were dead. It's a wonder any of them survived. Ed and his friend suffered major frostbite, Ed losing both of his feet, and his friend lost most of his fingers and toes. But they were alive.

I will never forget the patience of Ed's pregnant wife Sandy. She was a rock for the whole community during this ordeal. There was a quiet pall over the tiny town of Talkeetna as people tried to process and wait. Sandy and Ed were married in town and had made fast friends with everyone. Everyone did their best in the rescue; the weather was not their friend. Sandy delivered their first baby at Providence Hospital where Ed was recovering in the Burn Unit. The nurses videotaped the birth and ran it right up for Ed to watch! He had been on the phone with Sandy the whole time, it brought needed joy in a very difficult time for them.

Ed fell into deep depression afterwards; he and Sandy moved away from Alaska. They could not live the difficult rustic lifestyle offered in Talkeetna. Ed fought hard and came back as the first bilateral transtibial amputee to summit Mt. McKinley. He faced the mountain again after all the trauma he had gone through, and won. He battled through the depression and emotional pain writing a book about it titled *The Hill*. Ed went on to establish the High Exposure Foundation that assists amputees in the United States and Nepal. He attempted to climb Mt. Everest but was turned back with 3,000 feet to go due to weather. Ed was the first bilateral amputee to get medical clearance to fly commercial airlines. He continued his career and flew for American Airlines.

I was looking forward to reconnecting with him, but during my research, I found he had died. I was shocked. As he was training on Mt. Rainier in Washington for his next Everest attempt in 2002, Ed was killed by a falling rock. He was doing what he loved. He died living. I will always remember Ed for his sensitivity and sweet concern for people, and Sandy for her tremendous strength. They had three children. I had the privilege to sing at their joyful wedding in Talkeetna in the summer prior to the crash that changed so many people's lives.

While all this was going on with Ed's crash, Don was having his own difficult time with his plane. Pilots must stay sharp to avoid disaster. This was one of those times when the weather moved in without a moment's notice. While Don was doing the flybys over Kahiltna Pass he soon found himself on the other side of the pass from Talkeetna with no way back. Whiteout conditions blocked the way home. You do not fly in those conditions because of the disorientation it causes. Don called me on the phone from a Flight Service Station on the opposite side of the mountain, where he spent the night. He told me he was getting low on fuel but had enough to get home. Early in the morning Don was so eager to get back that he failed to check for winds aloft at high altitude. He took off and went up to 12,000 feet thinking he would just zip over the pass with no problem. The winds threw him off course and he developed a condition known as hypoxia from too little oxygen. Over 10,000 feet the air has less oxygen. Don began hallucinating, became lethargic, and didn't think clearly. By the time he realized he was in trouble, he was really in trouble. Flying around a 20,000-foot peak and not knowing where you are is concerning to say the least. He tried to plot his course as well as he could figure and then got on the radio and gave a "Mayday". With fuel running low, Don knew he needed to find a place to land but all he could see were clouds. It was totally "socked in" weather underneath him. He sent up a prayer and an equally frantic "Mayday," detailing his situation and where he thought he was. This mayday was heard back at the Air Taxi Service in Talkeetna. At that very moment a hole opened up in the clouds. It was his only chance. He put the nose of the plane down and spiraled into it. On the way down the pressure was so great the fuel bladders collapsed, choking off the gas flow to the engine of the Cessna 185. The engine sputtered and died, with Don feeling he was about to die. He wasn't the kind to give up easily as he kept the plane in a very tight circle, spinning and falling through the little opening in the clouds. Suddenly, he caught a glimpse of the snowy ground below and then he saw something he recognized—the tower at Rainey Pass Lodge! He landed the plane with a thump, throwing up snow in all directions, totally burying the plane. The plane was unscathed and so was he.

The caretaker at the lodge had heard the sound of an airplane descending and also heard the engine quit. He knew someone was in trouble. There was no sight or sound of the airplane as he started the snow machine and began a frantic grid pattern search. While hearing the snow machine methodically going back and forth Don exited the buried plane and trudged a mile to the lodge. He arrived before the caretaker, who gave him an enthusiastic welcome.

While Don was settling in at Rainy Pass, Talkeetna Air Taxi had heard the mayday call from 16,000 feet unknown location. Nothing else had been transmitted.

I got a call from Doug asking me to come in to the Air Taxi office. *Something's up, Doug has never asked me to come to the office before.* Walking in the office door, there sat Doug dejectedly shaking his head, "We don't what happened to Don, last we heard was a mayday. Ed and his people are still trapped on the mountain with the weather closing in again." Doug looked like the weight of the world was on his shoulders. He knew more than anyone what the men on McKinley faced.

We didn't know if Don was dead or alive. Fearful thoughts can crowd the peaceful heart, but I felt Don was alive and had quiet peace.

We heard from Don that afternoon. What a relief to learn he was safe! The Rainy Pass caretaker made a runway with his snow machine the next day and they got the hefty plane dug out of the snow. They found the fuel bladders collapsed from the pressure change, answering why the engine had quit on his steep spiral back to earth. Putting more fuel in solved the problem. Don's plane was a Cessna 185 on hydraulic wheel skis. It could take off from an airstrip on wheels or with the wheel skis pumped on they could take off and land on snow. Don made it home to everyone's relief.

OUTHOUSES AND OTHER ODDITIES

Outhouses are fascinating in Alaska. Cities and towns have organized infrastructure in place but villages do not have utilities. Everyone I knew in Talkeetna had an outhouse for a bathroom. Out of all housing structures, the outhouse was the most praised. Most outhouse seats are made of a hole cut in Styrofoam. This insulates in the cold and is warm after a few seconds of body heat. The Styrofoam prevents skin from freezing to the seat. It's a sad experience to be stuck to an outhouse seat. One person I know has a two-holed outhouse with lids, curtains on the windows, and magazines in a rack. Another friend had made a little part of the outhouse wall to resemble a window, curtains, and had a guest book to sign while sitting there. This was my mountain climbing brother's outhouse and he had many famous people sign in there!

    My favorite outhouse story comes from the time we lived in our first cabin, the one vacated by the five bachelors. Don had built the outhouse out of a hollow cottonwood tree by cutting a seven-foot segment, standing it upright over the hole, cutting a doorway and roofing it with a piece of tin. It was situated fairly close to the cabin, maybe ten or fifteen feet away. By the time I arrived on the scene, that outhouse was dirty and gross, with flies and fly larvae all over the inside. There was no door and that bothered me most. You never knew who might be peering in…I detested that thing! As I walked home later that summer day my friend Steve Mahay stopped me looking grim. "Did you hear the news?" he asked while watching me closely. I prepared myself immediately for the fact that our house had probably burned down. I replied, "No, I haven't heard anything." Steve's face was dead-pan serious as he said, "Your outhouse burned down." He had tried to break it to me gently, thinking I would probably be upset but I laughed. In fact, I laughed the rest of the two miles home, with tears streaming down my face.

    How does an outhouse burn down, you ask? That morning before I left for town, there were so many flies inside the outhouse I couldn't stand to sit there. They would buzz around and hit you on the butt, really annoying! Don said, "I'll fix it." He ran in the house to get a couple of cherry bomb firecrackers, (which every Alaskan home has sitting around the house year round) lit them, and threw them down the hole. It created a whole lot of smoke and out went the flies. That solved the problem, at least momentarily. It seems the cherry bombs did a lot more than eradicate the flies. The firecrackers started a poop fire down in the hole of our outhouse, and all that was left of our quaint little cottonwood tree outhouse was the tin roof and smoldering ashes. The wind was blowing right toward our cabin that day and we had just oiled the logs with a mixture of log oil and diesel fuel. It's a wonder it didn't burn the cabin down as well. Poor Don! His picky new wife did nothing but complain about that outhouse. Now that it was gone, I complained because we didn't have one!

When we finally got running water (at the next cabin) Don was the one who wanted an indoor toiler and hot shower, even more than I did! He just never said anything.

Earlier I mentioned with bad road conditions, the guys would simply hop out of their Datsun pickup, pick it up and walk it through deep muddy stretches? The road wasn't much better than that when I moved out there. In winter there wasn't a plowed road. We had to take snow machines or walk into town. We had a big Alpine that I could not use by myself because you had to light it on fire to get it started. Don would pour some gas in the carburetor, light a match, pull the starter rope hoping to get it going then blow out the fire. We did have another snow machine but with Don gone, it would never start for me, even after pulling and pulling on it. Don would come home and with one pull it started right up giving me a look like, *Why can't you do this?* I walked a lot or stayed home.

That first winter was dreadfully cold, I always bundled up causing me to walk stiffly from so many layers of clothing. One night coming home from church on the Alpine with Don, I was marveling at what a beautiful moonlit night it was as we skimmed the snow at forty below zero. Suddenly, the combination of the seat being too short and too slick caused me to slowly slip off the rear of the snow machine, gently laying me on my back in the snow. I discovered I had so many doggone clothes on, I couldn't get up. I lay there, looking up at the multitude of stars and thinking as I listened to Don roar off in the distance, *Wow this sure is pretty.* I lay there until he realized I was no longer sitting behind him and came back to get me. Women are such trouble for men in Alaska!

The boots I wore daily in the winter were called "moon boots" after the NASA moon landing boots. Don wore "bunny boots" which trapped warm air from your feet in between layers of boot, creating warm air pockets. Once, Don got a job on the North Slope but forgot his boots in Talkeetna. He was flying out of Anchorage and I had to get them to him. Lowell Thomas was flying back to Anchorage from Talkeetna in his Helio Courier, and I begged a ride. Lowell is a wonderful gentle Alaskan man, and he chuckled that Donnie needed his boots. I was heavily pregnant and we were almost to Anchorage. Lowell wanted to show me some stalls. (*No!* I was getting airsick!) Why is it that pilots want to show me how their plane stalls? Yes, I threw up in Lowell Thomas Jr.'s airplane. But I did get Don his boots before he left for the North Slope.

One of the first things a person notices about Alaska is that every vehicle has several dents in it or rust everywhere on it. (This quirk fits right in with the people who don't have walls or indoor plumbing.) When we were in Minnesota for our honeymoon, I couldn't believe all the beautiful cars—they were shiny, new, no dents or rust, and probably not paid for! But I didn't see any beat up trucks. I kinda missed that!

We owned a little Toyota Corolla (the same one I hauled the pigs in) and a $500 Ford truck. In winter, if our road had been plowed, we had places to go. Oil in our vehicles had to be heated up for the motor to start. The only way to heat the oil without electricity was to light a fire under them—literally! I remember looking out the plastic window and seeing fires blazing away under the vehicles and wondering if they were going to blow up—but they didn't. We were soon on our way. Some folks chose a safer, but more difficult method to assure their vehicle would start, by draining the oil every time they got home and bringing it inside for the night. Then in the morning, they would pour the warm oil back into the engine. With Don, it was always bonfire. With me it was whatever worked!

Any time that travel to other states is needed, it is referred to as a trip to the "Lower 48." One drawback to life in Alaska was the fact that all my relatives lived in the Lower 48 and consequently, trips to see them were expensive and few. The solution was to adopt family. My adopted aunt and uncle were Dennis and Millie Branham. Having no children of their own they came to our house every Christmas, Thanksgiving and Birthdays to enjoy the festivities. Dennis and Millie were another pair of tried and true Alaskans, owning and operating several hunting and fishing lodges over many decades. They were a wonderful, consistent part of my life growing up and beyond.

Unfortunately, I never knew either of my Grandfathers since both passed away before I was born. I met my maternal Grandmother, Mollie Dear Parker, only once at her home in Louisiana. My other Grandmother, Hattie Babb Hale, I saw a few times. Hattie was a preacher's wife and started every morning reading her Bible. I did get to see my aunt Hazel and uncle Bill. And my cousins Bill, Bob, and Marilyn on several trips. All of them were warm and welcoming to the "upper 49ers." It was always special to visit the family but we never got to spend enough time with them.

Whenever we traveled I met people that thought we lived in ice igloos. There was not a lot known about the mysterious forty-ninth state. Traveling to Alaska is like visiting another country. Growing up our fashion was usually behind the rest of the United States. Remember hot pants? By the time it was popular in Alaska, it was out of style in the Lower 48.

We have our wonderful Canadian neighbors to the East and Russia to the West. Recently, Sarah Palin was much mocked for a statement about being able to see Russia from her backyard, but it was a line made up by a comedian, not Sarah's words. During the Cold War Russia was a threat. Soviet fighter MIG's and bombers broke our airspace at least once a day, every day. Our fighters were scrambled on a daily basis. People kept emergency shelters for protection, rations, and weapons. It was real to us, Alaska could be invaded during that time. Russia is only one hundred fifty miles from Alaska. Alaska was even fired on and occupied by Japanese forces in WW II! Most people do not know that.

I would be terribly amiss if I did not mention the Bird House. It was situated right off the Seward Highway on Bird Creek, about halfway to Mt. Alyeska. Sadly, it is no more but here is the story. Always a good stopping place, large tour buses and visitors were drawn there by a huge brightly colored blue bird, sitting on a tiny cabin. The bar was small, three tables and three tree stump seats at the bar with business cards and ladies' panties (free drinks) tacked all over the walls. Because it was a popular stopping place for tourists, the minuscule bathrooms had the door hinges and handles on the same side. I had not been drinking but could not find my way out of that bathroom to save my life! My friend had to be dispatched to come find me and explain how to open the door! This proved to be entertaining for the owner and barkeepers. We left them keeping back a chuckle.

In the 1964 earthquake the floor had tilted a ten-degree angle up to the bar, much like my first cabin kitchen. People had to get a start on the sawdust and peanut shell floor to grab the bar and hang on. All this was terribly hard for me sober; I cannot imagine facing these challenges drunk. People did, every night. The owner eventually died in a plane crash in 1993, the bar burned down three years later from electrical problems, business cards, and dusty panties.

LAST THOUGHTS

The Alaska I grew up in has forever changed. All my friends from Talkeetna have running water and indoor toilets now. When I visited last I did not recognize the little town I lived in for thirteen years. Talkeetna in 2013 is still a village with an Honorary Mayor of Stubbs the cat; it has grown up and gone on. Anchorage is now a thriving modern city of over 300,000 people. When I was in high school it was only 68,000, and you knew everyone.

Some of the old landmarks still exist; a Bird House replica is at Chilkoot Charlie's bar in Anchorage. Gwennie's Old Alaskan Restaurant still serves Alaska size dishes. I would wish Alaska could stay the same, but no place does. I choose to playback the good old days. They truly were good times as well as hardship, as life is. Memories get sweeter as time passes.

This memory is not so sweet but still vivid: an old-fashioned gun battle happened over ownership of a woodpile "up the tracks" from Talkeetna. Two men who had a past of arguing and disagreements pulled weapons on each other at short range and starting shooting. One was dead on arrival, and the other lived but had a bullet right next to his aorta, he was air lifted to the hospital and lived. They were both shot six times. This supports my "Old West Theory". My theory is the pioneers of the Wild West expansion continued up to Alaska.

Alaskans are tough, independent, resilient people who live on the last frontier in America. I considered my parents Dr. George and Mary Hale so courageous to have ventured into such a demanding environment and make a life for themselves and their family. I am forever grateful that they did. I feel very fortunate to have grown up in such a tremendously unique place, and I benefit daily from the creativity and independence it fostered in me and my children. We will always love it, even though we no longer make it our home; only my son Andy still lives there. The older I get the farther south I venture!

Although it is quickly being settled and civilized, Alaska will always have its wild places, places that speak resoundingly to the heart. It can be harsh and unforgiving while bestowing wondrous gifts that lift the spirit and cause the heart to soar. I will be forever filled with the warmth of the people, the fascinating wildlife, and the enormity of landscape in its raw and unequaled splendor. There simply is no place like it.

Throughout my adventures there has been one friend I would be negligent not to mention. I would be aware as I talked to Smokey and walked in the woods of not being alone, like someone was with me and listening. There was someone with me, his name is Jesus and I came to know him when I was twenty. I was visiting a little church in Talkeetna when I met him and l have never been the same. I have hope. It was God that kept me and my family safe. It was Jesus that cared for me when no one else was there. He was.

I pray for you that you will be aware of the presence of God in your life, his love and concern for you. I encourage you to find a Bible preaching church and read the Bible so you can find the Lord in your life too! Ask God to guide you and be with you, he will!

Happy adventuring!
Nancy

Printed in the USA
CPSIA information can be obtained
at www.ICGtesting.com
LVHW021330110924
790643LV00014B/856